Corrupting Youth

The *Big Ideas for Young Thinkers Book Series* brings together the results of recent research about pre-college philosophy. There has been sizable growth in philosophy programmes for young people. The book series provides readers with a way to learn about all that is taking place in this important area of philosophical and educational practice. It brings together work from around the globe by some of the foremost practitioners of philosophy for children. The books in the series include single-author works as well as essay collections. With a premium placed on accessibility, the book series allows readers to discover the exciting world of pre-college philosophy.

Corrupting Youth

History and Principles of Philosophical Enquiry (PhiE)

Volume 1

Peter Worley
Series Editor: Thomas Wartenberg

ROWMAN & LITTLEFIELD
Lanham • Boulder • New York • London

Published by Rowman & Littlefield
An imprint of The Rowman & Littlefield Publishing Group, Inc.
4501 Forbes Boulevard, Suite 200, Lanham, Maryland 20706
www.rowman.com

6 Tinworth Street, London SE11 5AL, United Kingdom

British Library Cataloguing in Publication Information Available

Library of Congress Cataloging-in-Publication Data Is Available

Library of Congress Control Number: 2020951569

ISBN: 978-1-4758-5919-5 (cloth : alk. paper)
ISBN: 978-1-4758-5920-1 (pbk. : alk. paper)
ISBN: 978-1-4758-5921-8 (electronic)

♾™ The paper used in this publication meets the minimum requirements of American National Standard for Information Sciences—Permanence of Paper for Printed Library Materials, ANSI/NISO Z39.48-1992.

You can think and speak.

—Professor M.M. McCabe's
formulation of Parmenides' conditions
for dialectic (1982, 2015)

How can you own water really? It's always flowing in a stream, never the same, which in the stream of life we trace. Because life is a stream.

—*Ulysses*, James Joyce

Dedicated to Mary Margaret ('M.M.') McCabe and Catherine McCall

Contents

Foreword

Thomas Wartenberg (Series Editor)

It's a genuine pleasure to write a foreword to Peter Worley's wonderful book, *Corrupting Youth*. This book has two volumes. The first is more theoretical; the second, more practical. But both elements are woven into each volume.

Worley is the Co-Chief Executive Officer of the Philosophy Foundation, a registered charity in the UK. He has written numerous books and articles about teaching philosophy to young people and has been active in schools for many years. He brings his expertise in working with young people to *Corrupting Youth*, a book that brings together the many ideas he has developed during his career. It is an important contribution to the literature on philosophy for children and should be read by anyone interested in the theory and practice of philosophising with young people.

Practitioners of philosophy for and with children (P4wC) standardly assume that the theoretical roots of this educational practice are the pragmatic philosophy of, especially, John Dewey. Worley contests this view, tracing his own method – which he dubs *philosophical enquiry* (PhiE) – back to the Ancient Greeks. It is not unusual for philosophers to connect the practice of P4wC to Socrates' practice of questioning the citizens of Athens about important ethical concepts such as justice, morality and friendship.

Worley proceeds differently, tracing the roots of PhiE back to a range of Greek thinkers including Heraclitus, Parmenides, Plato and Aristotle. He sees these Greek thinkers as developing a method of inquiry that is a better foundation for working with young people than the standard Deweyian model.

Key here is the notion of *dialectic*, first articulated by Heraclitus. Although many of us are unsure what to make of a thinker who proposed that 'you cannot step into the same river twice', Worley demonstrates that a careful unpacking of the various fragments shows that Heraclitus' dialectical model of philosophy can provide excellent guidance for those interested in getting young children involved in philosophical discussions.

Heraclitus is just the first of the Greek thinkers who Worley discusses and uses to explain his own method for working with children. The thinker who figures most centrally in Worley's discussion is, as I have mentioned, Socrates – and with him Plato, Socrates' student whose dialogues show us the elements of Socrates' practice.

What emerges from Worley's examination of the ideas of the Greek philosophers is a model for doing philosophy with young people that is quite distinctive. Although it may seem that employing these philosophers to explain how one can best work with youths at the present time is needlessly complex, this is not the case at all. For we can see in the manner in which Socrates interacted with the youths in his own home of Athens gives us guidance on how to get young people to engage in philosophical discussions that are genuinely the product of their own understandings rather than a reflection of the beliefs of their teachers.

Worley is committed to the idea that young people have the ability to discuss philosophy. All that is required is a skillful facilitator who can help them pursue their own thoughts in a careful and controlled manner. These two volumes explain the basic assumptions and tactics that a facilitator needs to use to assist young people in discussing philosophy.

Anyone interested in understanding what is involved in getting children to discuss philosophy is well advised to read Worley's two-volume study. They will receive both a firm theoretical grounding in the practice and very clear advice about how best to proceed.

In our current difficult circumstances, it is all the more important for adults to assist children in thinking about the complex world in which they find themselves. Philosophy is one of the most important ways we have for thinking about our world. Worley's book is an excellent guide to use for those interested in helping children make sense of the complexities of the world they face.

—Thomas Wartenberg (series editor)

Preface

Facilitator: So, was Socrates a wise man?
Lennie (age 10): Yes, because he believed in truth and stood up for the truth.
Millie (age 10): Yes and no. *Yes* because, as Lennie said, he believed in the truth, but *no* because he got himself killed.

In Athens 2,500 years ago, the philosopher Socrates was put on trial by a jury of his peers and charged with 'corrupting the youths of Athens and believing in gods other than the city-approved gods'[1] (*Apology* 24b-c).[2] He defended himself, but was nevertheless found guilty, sentenced to death and subsequently executed.[3] This is often paraphrased to mean that he was put to death for inciting the young people of Athens to question, including questioning authority, and that this was frowned upon by certain powerful people. But, as is often the case, there is more to this story.

Those that convicted him probably did not expect him to die, but instead, to undergo an enforced exile. In the *Crito*,[4] Plato records how his friends arranged for Socrates to escape the city and to stay with friends outside of Athens. According to Athenian law he was also entitled to suggest an alternative punishment and the court would have expected him to do this. The *Crito* also records how Socrates refused to go into exile, despite all the arrangements having been made. He argued that, being an Athenian, he bore a duty to the city to see through any punishments conferred upon him, having benefited his whole life from the amenities the city had provided him. As for the alternative punishment, he treated that with disdain, suggesting that they provide him with free meals in the Prytaneum, where Olympian victors were honoured (*Apology* 36e-37a).

What happened to Socrates was inextricably linked to the volatile political situation at the time. He had, throughout the latter part of his life, associated with some key players in the downfall of democracy in Athens and the – albeit brief – implementation of the Spartan-controlled Thirty Tyrants, among them, notably, Critias and Alcibiades. As well as the more general questioning of accepted, received opinion, the charge of 'corrupting the youths of Athens', would have had a more specific meaning to the jury: the corruption of the young Alcibiades through his close friendship with Socrates. Not only was Alcibiades a traitor, working for the Spartans in the crippling war between Sparta and Athens, he was also crucial in the instigation of the Thirty Tyrants. Socrates was being blamed for how Alcibiades had turned out and for what he had done to Athens. Socrates was a scapegoat.

If we understand 'gods' to stand in for 'values', in the way Neil Gaiman's 'American Gods' (2001) do, then it is easy to see how Socrates expressed – and lived – values at odds with those of contemporary Athens. He was neither beautiful nor a model citizen, or, to use a known Greek expression at that time, he was not a good example of *kalokagathia* (from the Greek words *kalos*, 'beautiful', and *agathos*, 'virtuous').

He would have been expected, having completed his military service (for which he received honours), to have gone into political life. That he did not was deplored by many Athenians and it is thought by some that the following comment in Pericles' *Funeral Oration* reported by Thucydides (2009) was aimed at Socrates: 'We consider the man who takes no part in civic duties not as unambitious, but as useless' (*The Peloponnesian War* 2.40.2).

This story describes someone both loyal to and at odds with the city into which they were born. A good friend would be expected to be loyal but also to question and even to say the truth, though it may be painful (*parrhesia* in Greek), and it is this kind of relationship that Socrates seems to have had with his city. So, his relationship with Athens was, like that with his interlocutors in Plato's dialogues (Cooper 1997), a dialectical one: a back-and-forth, question-and-answer dialogue in search of wisdom.

Given that the city's patron deity was Athena, Socrates' desire for wisdom would, contrary to the charge against him, have been very much in line with the values expressed in and through her: she was the goddess of wisdom and the city's protector; the city of Athens took its name from her. Yet his compulsion to push that search passed the point of comfort for many powerful Athenian citizens put his wisdom into question (see Lennie and Millie's comments above).

Whether Socrates' project of engaging the young people of Athens in philosophical conversations was a corrupting one lies in whether we think that this kind of dialectical relationship with our own city, country, values and 'gods' is a healthy one. And it is this question that the book you now have in your hands asks its readers. For my part, I believe that it is an unhealthy state that forbids dialogue, questioning and any discomfort that may follow from this. If the encouragement of these forms of exchange is corrupting, then it is a 'virtuous corruption'; one worth defending, even dying for.

***

Currently, PhiE is not fully described in a single publication, so the aim of this book (Volumes 1 and 2) is to bring the method together from all its disparate sources into one publication. The emphasis of this book is to place PhiE firmly in the Socratic tradition and more explicitly than most other approaches to doing philosophy in schools and other settings. But it also expands PhiE's influences beyond Socrates to a broader ancient Greek tradition, including those that preceded him and those that followed, in both senses of the word 'follow'.

I often refer to 'pupils' and 'participants', sometimes interchangeably. *Pupils*, because much of my own experience of doing philosophy in the public sphere is in primary and secondary education. *Participants* is used to describe all those that have engaged in doing PhiE over the years, including, in addition to children between the ages of two and sixteen, prisoners, adults and young adults in community groups, patients in hospitals, healthcare professionals, employees in businesses, politicians, members of the general public, professional colleagues, undergraduates, graduates, postgraduates, teachers and lecturers. I've used whichever word, *pupil* or *participant*, seems to me most appropriate to the context, but in both cases I simply mean *those taking part in doing PhiE and who are not the facilitators*.

Due to space restrictions, there is some material I've had to leave out of these books, such as speaker management, rules and etiquette of talk, behaviour management, games and so on. Given that this book is a guide to dialectal philosophy, I've omitted that material which did not directly relate to the dialectical aspect of facilitating PhiE (see The Philosophy Foundation's blog for posts about classroom management). Also, you may have your own way of approaching these aspects and there is no single way to do these as part of PhiE. For those who are interested, I have written about these aspects in more detail in my other session-plan-oriented books especially *The If Machine* (Worley 2011, 2019b), *40 Lessons to Get Children Thinking* (Worley 2015b) and *100 Ideas for Primary Teachers: Questioning* (Worley 2019a).

In Appendix 5 (Vol. 2) I have provided, in one place, a helpful table of the key moves a facilitator will need to have at their fingertips when facilitating a PhiE or other dialectically focused enquiry. The table gives the move name, a description, the type of move it is and the page numbers where you can read about it in more detail. I've also done some full transcriptions (with notes) of PhiE sessions, available for free download from this online supplement for *Corrupting Youth*: https://www.philosophy-foundation/resources. 'The Sirens' session is based on the chapter from *The If Odyssey* (2012) and has been presented as a good representative example of a standard PhiE session using the basic procedural model (see page 7 in Vol. 2) and working with a typical class in a state school in the UK with a higher than average number of Pupil Premium students.[5] They were the *control* group in the research TPF ran with King's College London looking into metacognitive and critical thinking skills development in PhiE (Worley & Worley 2019c).

The 'Can you choose your own beliefs?' session is the final session that was run for the *intervention* research group: another class in the same school as the control group. This session models how to run the *extended thinking programme* (in Vol. 2). Both volumes will make a good deal more sense when read against the background of full, classroom PhiE sessions.

All the exchanges in this book between facilitator and pupil-participants are taken from actual conversations in the classroom, either from memory, written accounts from the time, photographs of whiteboards with children's comments on or recordings and transcripts. I have noted where they have been taken from transcripts.

In principle, PhiE is very simple. You ask a good question (see 'Heraclitus' on page 14–17 and 'Questions in PhiE' on page 13 of Vol. 2), and then you allow the *dialectical triangle* to do its thing: allow group members *to think, to speak* and *to listen* (see page 2 of Vol. 2). Use the *if-ing, anchoring* and *opening-up* method (see page 41 in Vol. 2) to manage the dialectical aspect of the discussion while still giving space (absence on page 67 and OQM on page 71) to the thinking, the speaking and the listening. And, in a nutshell, that's it! It is true that there is more complexity to PhiE, but only in *how* to implement these aspects *well*, not in doing much more, additionally.

I remain somewhat tentative about whether PhiE is a definitively distinct approach to doing philosophy from P4/wC, so I will leave it to you, the reader, to decide for yourself. Much of what you will find in this book is certainly supplementary to a good deal of P4/wC practice, given that it too is largely an oral/aural approach to doing philosophy.[6]

As for the structure of this volume, following a general introduction to PhiE, where I've said something about the origins, inspirations and preliminary concerns, Part One addresses the important question, for a book about doing dialectical philosophy, of what philosophy is, or, at least, given how problematic this question is, how it is best understood from the point of view of PhiE. It also addresses, at some length, what is meant by *dialectic* in PhiE, its ancient Greek origins and developments from Heraclitus through to Aristotle.

Part Two outlines the core values of PhiE by way of analogy with the core values of the ancient Greeks, as identified by Edith Hall in her book *The*

Ancient Greeks: Ten Ways They Shaped the Modern World (2015), which, fortuitously, afforded a 'perfect fit' with PhiE.

Part Three takes the reader through a tour of the key pedagogical principles of PhiE – including the keystone ideas of *absence* and *open questioning mindset* (OQM) – as well as providing examples of the historical precedents for the principles from key primary source materials (mainly Plato's dialogues).

Volume 2 looks at the practical aspects of PhiE that have been built on the foundations laid out in Volume 1.

A LITTLE BACKGROUND

Given that this book refers a great deal to the ancient philosophers, it will be helpful to get a little background information at the outset to get a sense of the timelines of the philosophers and their chronological relationship to one another.

Philosophy in Western Europe is often traced back to the ancient Greeks, beginning with the pre-Socratic philosophers, so named because they lived before Socrates, who died c. 399 BCE at around about the age of 70. The first of the pre-Socratics was Thales and he lived during the 6th century BCE, so this should give you a sense of the time scale. It is also helpful to know that Socrates was the teacher of Plato (427–347 BCE), Plato the teacher of Aristotle (384–322 BCE) and Aristotle the teacher of Alexander the Great (356–323 BCE), not a philosopher, but a significant enough historical figure to help the reader orientate herself.

This tells us that 'the three biggies' of ancient Greek philosophy, Socrates, Plato and Aristotle, were around at the end of the Golden Era of Athens and (Aristotle) at the birth of the Hellenistic period, where the Greeks came under Macedonian rule. Then, through Alexander's love of everything Greek, Hellenic (that is, *Greek*) culture was taken much further afield than the Aegean.

Socrates never wrote down his philosophical ideas, so when he was accused of 'corrupting the minds of the young and preaching gods other than the city-approved gods' by some influential Athenian citizens, found guilty and put to death, Plato was sufficiently moved to write an account of his teacher's trial (see Plato's *Apology*). Plato went on to write a huge corpus of dialogues, featuring Socrates as the main interlocutor, and it is chiefly through Plato's 'Socratic' dialogues that we receive a picture of Socrates the philosopher. And, though there are other existing accounts of Socrates by Aristophanes and Xenophon, Plato's are the most extensive. Plato's 'dialogues' are written as dramatic encounters between, usually, Socrates and other Athenians (and visitors to Athens) in and around the marketplace – or 'agora' (see page xxx) –

of Athens. However, Plato's agenda seems to have been far more than to merely record the historical Socrates, it is also literary, dramatic, philosophical and political.

Traditionally, the early dialogues – the so-called 'Socratic dialogues' – are thought to be, more-or-less, historical accounts of Socrates whereas the later dialogues are thought to represent, usually with Socrates as a mouthpiece, Plato's own philosophical ideas. This tradition, however, is widely disputed, so the historical and the literary 'Socrateses' are ineluctably blurred. When I refer to Socrates and his methods, I refer to the 'Socrates' we get through Plato's dialogues, real or otherwise. I do not need to assume that the account is historically accurate or true to be able to draw upon this account as a philosophical source and inspiration, but it helps to know this so that the reader is not confused by the close references to both Plato and Socrates and their methods.

—Peter Worley, February 2020, London, England

NOTES

1. http://www.perseus.tufts.edu/hopper/text?doc=Perseus%3Atext%3A1999.01.0169%3Atext%3DApol.%3Asection%3D24b.

2. All references to Plato are to Cooper 1997 unless otherwise stated.

3. For this story, see the dialogues commonly known as 'The Last Days of Socrates', which include *Euthyphro*, *Apology*, *Crito* and *Phaedo*. For a fuller biography of Socrates, see in the bibliography *Socrates in Love: The Making of a Philosopher* by Armand D'Argour (2019) or *The Hemlock Cup: Socrates, Athens and the Search for the Good Life* by Bettany Hughes (2011).

4. A very short dialogue and so a nice place to start reading Plato.

5. This term refers to pupils on low income.

6. For differences between PhiE and P4/wC see: Tim Sprod, '(2) Book Review – 40 Lessons to Get Children Thinking: Philosophical Thought Adventures across the Curriculum', accessed 27 February 2020, https://www.researchgate.net/public ation/321880957_Book_review_-_40_lessons_to_get_children_thinking_Philosoph ical_thought_adventures_across_the_curriculum; Mihaela Frunza, '"Philosophy in Action" in the Texts and Practices of Peter Worley', *Studia Universitatis Babeş-Bolyai Philosophia* 64, no. 3 (2019), pp. 25–40.

Acknowledgements

I started doing philosophy in schools in 2002. I had been working as a peripatetic guitar teacher in primary schools in South East London and had observed what I called the 'ensemble effect' in my guitar groups: that a group of children could produce something greater than each individual child. I had also been training to do something that was then called *philosophical counselling* (more commonly referred to today as *philosophical consultancy*) and for which I must thank my trainers and mentors Tim LeBon, David Arnaud and Antonia Macaro of the Society of Philosophical Practice (SPP). As a result, I completed a course in Rogerian counselling as well as undertaking a masters in ethical philosophy to complement the BA degree in general philosophy I already had.

All of this came together when I was offered an opportunity to develop a philosophy programme at two of the primary schools in which I was already teaching guitar (my thanks go to head teachers Kathy Palmer and Cynthia Eubanks OBE for this opportunity). A year or so after first beginning the programme I was introduced to P4/wC ('philosophy for/with children') by Susan Wright of the SPP, and I subsequently attended a Sapere training course in the UK with Joanna Haynes and Karin Murris, where I was introduced to the Community of Inquiry (CoI) pedagogy of Pierce, Dewey and Lipman/Sharp.

It was through guitar teaching that I received my pedagogical apprenticeship, a combination of learning 'on the job' by trial and error, reading around, imitating my own guitar teacher (thanks to Luke Dunlea for being such a great model), receiving informal voluntary training from the music service for which I worked (my thanks for this go to my mentors Paula Kitson-Moore MBE and James Thomas), as well as preparing for a professional Diploma with Trinity in instrumental teaching.

My books, and their format, was a convergence of a series of inspirations from the early days of my doing philosophy in schools (and seeking out the scarce resources), notably Robert Fisher's . . . *for Thinking* books (*Stories* . . . , *Poems* . . . , *Games* . . . , and *Values* . . . [1997, 2001]), Stephen Law's *The Philosophy Files* (2011), and from much earlier, the 'choose-your-own-adventure' *Fighting Fantasy Gamebooks* of Steve Jackson and Ian Livingstone (1982), particularly the use of the second-person voice and choices for the reader, and the role-playing game *Dungeons and Dragons* by E. Gary Gygax and Dave Arneson, which treats gamers as active agents within co-created stories (1974, 1977, 1978, 1981, 1983).

In addition to all this, I also drew upon the figure of Socrates, not only as a philosophical mentor but also as a teacher. I understood from a very early stage of my teaching the importance of questioning, and I had learned a good deal about how to do this from my reading of Socrates at university, in particular, Plato's *Meno* dialogue – required reading for any teacher as far as I'm concerned. There were two principles that I derived from my ancient Greek teacher in the *Meno*: *teach by questioning as often as possible*, and *teach towards the unknown from the known*.

I first started to develop these ancient ideas further, and what I perceived to be their important relationship with education today, in a *Times Educational Supplement* (TES) competition-piece in 2008 entitled *Tomorrow's Teacher: Learning from the Past* (see bibliography for link) for which I was awarded a runner-up prize. The publication of this short think-piece put me in touch with Dr Fiona Leigh (UCL), who, having similar interests, had recently published a piece called 'Platonic Dialogue, Maieutic Method and Critical Thinking' (2007). It was Fiona who introduced me to the work of Prof. Mary Margaret 'M.M.' McCabe (KCL) and her keystone paper (certainly to this book) *Is Dialectic as Dialectic Does?* (2006, 2015).

I began a PhD at King's College London in 2009 under the supervision of both Fiona and M.M. in *Plato's pedagogy*. It was M.M. who would later recommend I become a Visiting Research Associate at KCL in 2015, which led to an ongoing relationship with the King's College philosophy department and our joint research project with Dr Ellen Fridland between 2016 and 2018 (Worley & Worley 2019c).

An early *Philosophy Foundation* event in 2010[1] based around a re-enactment of Monty Python's *philosophers' football match* put us in touch with Dr Catherine McCall with whom, it turned out, I shared a great many values and outlooks. We met and became friends around the time of the publication of her book *Transforming Thinking* (McCall 2009), but more than through the book, Catherine's influence came from the many conversations we had over the phone, at my home and at SOPHIA meetings, and it was Catherine

I followed as president of SOPHIA in 2014. We both share a commitment to ensuring that the *philosophy* in 'philosophical enquiry' remains genuinely philosophical.

I met the inimitable Pieter Mostert at the ICPIC conference of 2015 in Cape Town, South Africa. He introduced me to 'Clean Language Therapy' (Sullivan and Rees 2008) with which PhiE, the method described in this book, shares a good deal of principles and strategies. But, again, it was through many conversations with Pieter that his influence can be felt, sometimes (as with Catherine) in the extent to which we disagree as much as our agreement.

And thank you to my friend and editor of this book, Tom Wartenberg, for the support and conversations in and around this book and doing philosophy with children, and through whom the influence of Gareth Matthews is felt.

But, perhaps most of all, thanks must go to all at *The Philosophy Foundation* over the past ten plus years for the team's intellectual, pedagogical and professional commitment to the cause: bringing genuine philosophy to as many children and groups as possible, but particularly to those who might not otherwise get the opportunity to encounter philosophy. Within the team, a special thanks to the development of PhiE must go to Steve Hoggins, Steven Campbell-Harris, Miriam Cohen Christofidis, Andy West, Andrew Day, Rob Torrington, David Birch, Joe Tyler, Jennifer Wright and Georgina Donati.

I would like to thank Mark Vernon for helpful comments on the original manuscript. Other notables who have supported or influenced me and the work of *The Philosophy Foundation* include Michael Hand, Peter Adamson, Angie Hobbs and A.C. Grayling CBE (both of whom are honorary patrons), Josh Forstenzer (my current PhD supervisor), Laura D'Olimpio, Caroline Schaffalitzky de Muckadell, Arie Kizel, Susan Gardner, Roger Sutcliffe, Darren Chetty, Grace Lockrobin, Tim Sprod, Lynda Dunlop, Steve Williams, Jason Buckley, James Garvey, Julian Baggini, Ian and Lorraine Worley, Joc and Chris Swinn; and the trustees (current and former): Truda Spruyt, Jonathan Douglas, John Skelton, Cathy Tupman, Andy Russell, Andrew Flynn, Shalani Sequeira, Rebecca Urang, Cat Pamplin, Jasna Vrdoljak, Georgina Eilbeck and Suzy Deadman; our patrons, who include in addition to Angie Hobbs, A.C. Grayling and Catherine McCall: Robin Ince, Anthony Seldon, Nigel Warburton, Stephen Law, the late Python, Terry Jones – especially his p.a. Deborah Lyons; and, finally, our newest patron, Amia Srinivasan.

Of course, my heartfelt, eternal thanks go to Emma Worley (who was awarded an MBE for services to innovation in the 2020 New Year Honours), still my (and TPF's) *sine qua non*; more specifically, thanks to Emma for proofreading, structural suggestions and critical discussion that helped shape the book.

NOTE

1. When the charity was known as 'The Philosophy Shop' and was a Community Interest Company.

Introduction to PhiE

As well as having a range of influences (see 'Acknowledgements' on page xxi) and a concern to preserve the *philosophical* aspect of philosophy with children, there was also a kind of evolution-through-environment that helped shape PhiE – the method of doing dialectical philosophical enquiry described in this book – and that helped distinguish it from other practices. Since 2001, I have worked in schools in South East London in the UK and many of them have a high proportion of Pupil Premium students (see footnote 5 on page xx), which in the UK is an indication of the high levels of poverty in the borough.

This meant that many of the schools I worked in were 'challenging' schools, and many of the children struggled with anything that failed to engage them immediately. This ruled out some of the 'basics' I had learnt from my P4/wC[1] training. The picture books would often result in children disengaging and becoming disruptive while the picture was being shown to the children on the other side of the classroom. The procedures of the 10-step model[2] were too time-consuming to maintain the group's interest so that by the time the enquiry had been reached it was too late: I had lost them.[3]

I noticed that the two most engaging aspects of a session were direct storytelling (thanks to a recommendation from Robert Fisher in his *Stories for Thinking* [1997] to learn the stories by heart and tell them), and the discussion of their own ideas during an enquiry. This meant that I had to develop an approach that was strong on storytelling and that got the class to the enquiry as quickly as possible and that ensured the question was good enough to maintain their philosophical interest. Having the children choose their own question according to the 10-step model would often result in questions that not everyone was interested in, as well as questions that were often not sufficiently philosophical.

I tried many things and made notes on what worked and what didn't. I didn't know it then, but the question-type I identified as the best for doing philosophy was good for good reasons (see 'Dialectic' on page 12). The basic approach would begin with my presenting some kind of engaging *stimulus* to the group, something I learnt from standard P4/wC practice, such as a story, an activity, a puzzle, a thought-experiment, a performance, an experience, an image or a film.

Departing from standard P4/wC practice, this was followed with a well-chosen and well-structured question, prepared in advance, to start the class thinking about some philosophical aspect or aspects raised by the stimulus (see 'The Task Question' on page 13 in Vol. 2). But, of course, this had been done before![4]

As with PhiE, the Socrates we find in Plato's dialogues (see page xix) would usually begin a dialogue by responding to some kind of stimulus often presented in a 'frame' to the philosophical discussion. For instance, in the *Euthyphro*, Socrates meets the character Euthyphro at the law courts, and the 'real-life stimulus' for the main question 'What is piety?' is the fact that Euthyphro is there to prosecute his father for impiety. Once the question had been asked, Socrates would then facilitate an exploration and investigation of the question, attending to the dialectical demands along the way by a process of question-and-answer.

The strong resemblance of Plato's dialogues to PhiE invited me to consider in more depth what PhiE owes to Socrates and Plato. In some cases, the methods developed, such as the *Hokey Kokey* method (see page 76 in Vol. 2), were self-consciously built on Platonic/Socratic principles (in the case of *Hokey Kokey*, the movement between the *concrete* – 'Is it pious, Euthyphro, to prosecute your own father?' – and the *abstract* – 'What is piety?'), while other cases, such as *either-or-the-if*, were identified much later on as having correspondence in Plato or in his intellectual ancestors such as Heraclitus and Parmenides or his intellectual descendants (particularly Aristotle), all of whom had something important to contribute to the development of dialectical philosophy and to how it is understood and practised in PhiE.

What resulted in the high level of convergence, even when the influence was not direct, was the shared interest in *attending to the demands of dialectical philosophy*, that is, the logical, sequential, inference-based thinking done through question-and-answer conversations.

I decided to take a closer (and hopefully a fresh) look at the primary sources – and, although I have a smattering of ancient Greek, in most cases, through translations – to see what the direct influences, correspondences and convergences were between PhiE and the ancient philosophers. The extent of the correspondence astounded me! I believe that PhiE owes a much greater debt to the practice and theory of the ancients than it does to the usually credited American Pragmatists and their offspring (Peirce, Dewey, Lipman). This book is the product of that closer look.

***

In her book, *The Ancient Greeks: Ten Ways They Shaped the Modern World*, Edith Hall says,

> . . . the most important legacy left by Plato is the composition of philosophical reasoning in an open-ended dialogue form. It forces readers to read, to agree or disagree with Socrates, to think the issues through for themselves. Plato's texts demonstrate in practice how thinking and argument is a dialectical process: people who disagree can make progress toward understanding each other's positions if they continue their dialogue indefinitely and do not close it down. The Socratic dialogue, as recorded by the Athenian Plato, has had an incalculable influence, not only on methods of teaching but on the theory and practice of democracy. (Hall 2015, p. 157)

The two volumes of this book, then, present a modern pedagogical approach to facilitating *informal dialectical philosophical enquiry* (PhiE) based on principles, methods and techniques given to us by (or developed from) the ancient Greeks, from Heraclitus through Parmenides, Socrates, Plato and Aristotle in particular. The focus of this book is philosophy in schools (as that is the predominant experience of the author), but PhiE is a method that works with any group of people aiming to pursue better understanding towards truth through dialectical philosophical enquiry primarily outside (but also within) academia.

When I use the term *dialectic* (about which much more on page 12), as I shall a great deal in this book, I mean it in a sense closer to what is meant by the ancient Greeks than the later meaning associated with Hegel (though Hegel also has a role to play in the development of PhiE – see pages 5–6 in Vol. 2). In ancient Greek, *dialectic* means 'through speech' and refers to the question-and-answer approach to doing philosophy made popular through Plato's portrayal of Socrates in his dialogues. Although, it is worth noting, that Diogenes Laertius, in his *Lives of the Eminent Philosophers* – 3rd century CE – said that Protagoras was the first to practise this style of philosophical questioning, but unfortunately, there is no record of him doing so.

Whereas Hegel had something much more abstract in mind, such as the movement of history itself, the Greeks used it to describe a kind of back-and-forth in actual conversation between people. This much more concrete sense is how I generally mean *dialectic* in this book. Philosophical dialectic, however, does demand a little more than mere question-and-answer interplay for it to be considered a systematic, rigorous discipline so it is not just idle chatter. My own working definition of *dialectic* is as follows: *the systematic (logical and sequential) investigation of opinions through inferential question-and-answer conversations with others or with oneself* (see pages 12–25, 47 and 76 for more on this).

So, why *dialectical* philosophy in particular? 'Philosophy' is one of those words that resists singular definition and many people have a different definition of what exactly philosophy is (see 'What is philosophy?' on page 1). This means that while I do not *reduce* philosophy *only* to dialectical method, I do think this way of understanding philosophy (the logical, conceptual aspect of inference-making through conversation) is necessary to doing philosophy as well as being something that can be done by children, and something that can be spoken of and taught.

So, rather than claiming that this is the *only* way to conceive of doing philosophy, the dialectical aspect of philosophy is the aspect I have chosen to *focus on* for the purposes of describing a pedagogical method of doing philosophy with non-philosophers through conversation. So, while dialectic is not identical with philosophy, it being a method that allows for philosophical enquiry, dialectic is a necessary part of doing philosophy though it is not sufficient.

One may also be concerned that this dialectical approach to doing philosophy, being drawn from the ancient Greeks, is therefore *Euro-centric*. PhiE can be done (and in most cases, *it is*) without any mention of the ancient Greeks at all, in fact, one may use stimuli drawn from any cultural or philosophical tradition. Being dialectical, it is concerned with the structure of inference-making, something shared by many cultures and languages around the world that is found within many philosophical traditions. *Inference-making* ('If . . . then . . .'), *challenges to inferences* ('Just because . . . doesn't necessarily mean that . . .'), and *reason-giving* ('. . . because . . .') are the nuts, the bolts and the hinges of a truth-preserving discourse on which there is no single cultural monopoly.

Pierre Hadot (2002) says that the philosophical thought of 'Socrates, Pyrrho, Epicurus, the Stoics, the Cynics and the Sceptics . . . correspond to constant, universal models which are found, in various forms, in every civilisation, throughout the various cultural zones of humanity'. Quoting J.-L. Solere, Hadot says, 'the ancients were perhaps closer to the [East][5] than we are'. Sometimes, logical reasoning is seen as a distinctively Western cultural preserve, but the paradoxes of Heraclitus, for instance, sometimes resemble the paradoxes of Lao Tzu, Chuang Tzu or Zen Buddhism.

As Julian Baggini points out in his book *How the World Thinks* (2018), these writers (e.g., Tzu 1974; Tzu 2006; Senzaki 2000) do not reject traditional logic in their apparent contradictions, nor do they rely on a completely different kind of logic, they merely take the emphasis away from logical analysis that is so central to Western and particularly anglophone philosophy. Most of these so-called paradoxes play on equivocations and ambiguities, thereby exploiting and playing with traditional logic rather than flouting or rejecting it outright.

In addition, PhiE says nothing about what ideas will be brought into the discussions for consideration within dialectical structures, nor does it put any limit on the kinds of responses and contributions beyond inference-making structures, other than its having something to do with what is being discussed. The content and kind of response is determined by the participants, and they, depending on where PhiE is being practised, may well represent many different cultures and therefore different ways of thinking.

So, a child taking part in a PhiE may well contribute in ways associated with different philosophical traditions: she may contribute in a logical way, or in a more interpretative way, or she may even draw upon her own experiences or religious understanding and knowledge (see 'What is philosophy?' on page 1 for more on these distinctions). There are no *rules* about what kind of philosophy is done. That it is *dialectical philosophy* means only that the facilitator will ask students to say *why* they said what they said, to *explain* themselves more and to invite participants to *critically engage* with each other and to consider, inferentially, *what they think follows from what and why*. Beyond that, the philosophy is the philosophy the group makes, but without it transmogrifying into something else entirely (PSHE, SEAL, circle time, etc.)

Further to this, it would be very difficult to *stop* children responding to questions and to each other with these kinds of inferential structures. This is because it is natural for children in a UK or US school to use these structures and it would take a great deal of censorship and control to stop the children from using them. That they use these structures may be a result of the particular education they are already receiving (and this may indeed be Euro- or Anglo-centric in some way) and it may also be more hardwired and less culturally specific, but either way and wherever this kind of logical thinking has come from, PhiE allows facilitators to respond with a kind of facilitation that invites pupils to go a little further with these already learnt units ('nuts', 'bolts' and 'hinges') of thought.

PhiE is therefore a minimally *prescriptive* approach, it works on the assumption that children *already* think and express themselves using these basic structures, the PhiE facilitator simply aids them to be able to do so with greater *clarity*, *depth* and *precision*.

Building from the concept of *xenia* (or 'friendship of the guest' – see page 39), though the refined version of dialectical philosophy is Greek in origin, it welcomes the 'stranger': it welcomes diverse cultures, beliefs, customs and perspectives, with one caveat – that all of these (including its own practices and working assumptions – see pages 63–66) may become objects of critical, philosophical investigation. Though I believe this *critical assumption* to be a value shared by many cultures around the world, if it makes PhiE Euro-centric, then it is an aspect of European culture worth celebrating and defending.

As with many other ancient Greek philosophers, but particularly Socrates and those that came after him, Socrates' central philosophical interest was pursuing the practical question, 'How should I live?'. Coming after the pre-Socratic interest in cosmological matters, you might say that Socrates turned the telescope inward, away from the stars and towards the soul. This meant that philosophers following him were concerned with practical matters, with life and living it. To see this, just consider Socrates' most famous saying: 'The unconsidered life is no human life'.

This is usually translated as 'The unexamined life is not worth living', but I will use my colleague Pieter Mostert's translation of 'bios' as 'human life' and replacing the usual 'unexamined' with 'unconsidered', to avoid the negative connotations of our school exam culture, and to concur with what I say on page 28 (in Vol. 2) about the centrality of the word 'consider' in PhiE communities.

So, with this 'Socratic revolution', Socrates was inviting *anyone* to the philosophical table. He probably didn't have young children (or women – apart from the notable exceptions of Diotima in *Symposium* and Aspasia in *Menexenus* – or slaves, or non-Greeks for that matter) in mind, but, despite his particular cultural assumptions, his invitation extends, *de facto*, to all who are capable of whatever is needed to be able to philosophise (see page 54), to anyone who might have a vested interest in life and how it can best be lived, or anyone interested in attaining a greater understanding of things, of ourselves and each other.

At the risk of anachronism, we might even want to say, in our post-Enlightenment world of universal human rights, that the right to education extends to *anyone capable* of this kind of dialogic exchange *so that* they may *engage* in this kind of democratic exchange – why we might think of the right extending to people but not cats (see page 54), and why, today, we might extend that right beyond enfranchised, Greek males.

The idea that philosophy is for every person and that philosophical questions can and should be pursued by anyone, using the ordinary language they have at their disposal, was one of Socrates' great innovations regarding the practice of philosophy. Famously, Socrates conducted his philosophical investigations with young men in the Athenian *agora*, or, 'marketplace'. Following Hannah Arendt (1977/1978), the term 'agora' may stand for any place where philosophy is conducted outside of the academy: schools, prisons, pubs, hospitals, places of work, churches and so on. On this understanding, PhiE's commitment is to bring philosophy to the *agora*.

Aristotle took this practical aspect further to develop an entire, and still highly regarded and influential, system of ethics based around the goal of *eudaemonia*. Literally meaning 'well-attended spirit', this word is sometimes translated as 'happiness'. A key difference, though, between how we and the ancient Greeks thought of happiness is that we tend to think of it as *subjective* ('Whatever does it for you!'), whereas the Greeks thought of these things more *objectively*, perhaps how we might think of something like physical health – what makes you healthy or unhealthy is not a matter of personal preference, but then, neither was happiness for the Greeks.

Another key difference is that happiness for a modern person is a *feeling* or *sensation* rather than a way of being (*ethos*). That means that, as well as being subjective, it is ephemeral and fleeting. For a modern person, if you *feel* unhappy, you *are* unhappy, but for a Greek, one could feel unhappy (perhaps because of an event such as a bereavement) while at the same time be happy, generally, in one's life. For the Greeks happiness could only be understood in the context of a whole life.

Understood within this Greek concept of *eudaemonia*, education should therefore be holistic. This asks for a radical shift in our modern tendency, away from thinking about education as *extrinsic*, where we see the pupil as nothing more than a producer or worker, towards a more *intrinsic* education of well-being and personal development, which, when understood this way, results in conferring extrinsic benefits as a 'happy' consequence.

A better translation of *eudaemonia*, then, is 'flourishing'. And if, as Aristotle did, we consider contemplation *at least* to be an important part of what it is to be human (for him it was the *defining* feature); and if we consider education to be, as many today do, the soil in which the soul takes root and grows, then we might argue for philosophy – the art and the science of contemplation – in schools as part of a rounded curriculum on the basis that it is an important condition, not just for *growth* in a minimal sense, but *flourishing* in an optimal sense: so, not just *becoming*, but *becoming the best you can be*. To put this in more up-to-date terminology, understood in this way, doing philosophy becomes part of the sum of conditions that enables *self-actualisation* (Goldstein 1993; Rogers 1961; Maslow 1943) to be possible (see notes on 'Autonomy' and 'Excellence' on pages 34 and 41).

One way to understand flourishing or self-actualisation is to see it as an act of self-creation. Pierre Hadot, in his book *What Is Ancient Philosophy?* says:

> The [ancient Greek] philosophical school thus corresponds, above all, to the choice of a certain way of life and existential option which demands from the

individual a total change of lifestyle, a conversion of one's entire being, and ultimately a certain desire to be and to live in a certain way'. (2002)

And in *Republic* (Book VII), Plato has Socrates say:

> . . . the power to learn is present in everyone's soul and . . . the instrument with which each learns is like an eye that cannot be turned around from darkness to light without turning the whole body . . . then education is the craft concerned with doing this very thing, this turning around, and with how the soul can most easily and effectively be made to do it. It isn't the craft of putting sight into the soul . . . education takes for granted that sight is there but that it isn't turned the right way or looking where it ought to look, and it tries to redirect it appropriately. (Cooper 1997)

The twist in this tale is that there is no 'bible' to turn to or philosopher that can provide a satisfactory single account of the right way to live, despite the efforts of numerous ancient philosophical schools that tried to do this such as the Stoics, the Cynics, the Sceptics, the Epicureans and so on. As the philosopher Alexander Nehamas points out in his book *The Art of Living: Socratic Reflections from Plato to Foucault*, philosophy, at the same time as being about an existential choice of a way of life is also the *way* one creates, often in conjunction with others, what that choice is and what it entails: 'To imitate Socrates is therefore to create oneself, as Socrates did', says Nehamas (1998).

This is what, according to Hadot and Nehamas, separates Socrates from the other ancient 'Schools': he was not a *dogmatist*; perhaps his only injunctions come down to this: 'Think for yourself' and: 'Create yourself'.

So, PhiE is not asking children to reflect and reason their way to becoming 'good citizens' as our generation might understand it (i.e., kind, thoughtful, democratic, tolerant and so on), it is inviting the children – and therefore the next generation – to autonomous thought (albeit in relation to others – see 'Autonomy' on page 34) as a first step towards self-creation, towards something you or I may consider better, but equally, perhaps not. The cherished ideals of our generation (democracy among them) may well be among those things 'up for grabs', and if that is the case, we should do what we can to ensure that the next generation do not stumble blindly into a new set of values, but approach them carefully, reflectively and constructively without instructing them what they should value.

A practical reason why Plato and Socrates (and their predecessors) are placed at the centre of PhiE is because there is a *pedagogy* that emerges from what is modelled by Plato, through Socrates, in his dialogues, standing on the shoulders of Heraclitus and Parmenides. Usually, when commentators talk about Plato and education, they refer to his explicit recommendations for a curriculum, primarily in the *Republic* (Book VII) but also other places. However, we should look, not at what he preaches, but primarily at what he *practices* in the dialogues, and what he practices is sometimes at odds with what he preaches.

Among other things, this book is an attempt to outline the implied pedagogies that emerge from reading Plato and Aristotle, directing the reader both to the relevant and to the corresponding historical sources, sometimes moving outside of Plato and Aristotle. More than merely *identifying* pedagogy in Plato et al., it is a *recommendable pedagogy*, one that not only is *able* to be done in classrooms today but, with a few tweaks and qualifications, also *should be*, given how it promotes the art and science of autonomous contemplation and flourishing.

There is one significant way that PhiE differs from Socratic approaches. That is in the *redirection* of the driving force in the enquiries. In the Socratic dialogues, it is Socrates who takes the lead with the structure of the discussion, what question is pursued and what much of the content is, even when the content is supposedly coming from his interlocutors. This is because Socrates asks many *leading questions* (see pages xxxiv and 69 in Vol. 1 and 57 in Vol. 2) of the form, 'Is it not that . . . ?' or 'Is it A or B?' or 'Do you not think . . . ?' in which he presents ideas in such a way that leaves his interlocutors with little option other than assent or denial (in most cases, they assent with 'Certainly', 'Necessarily' and so on). The readiness with which they offer assent to many of his suggestions often leaves the reader somewhat frustrated (see my comments on page 3) that Socrates' interlocutors do not challenge him more than they do.

This method of composition could have a *dialectical* aim that Plato wants his readers to properly engage with the issues, so he leaves the challenging to the reader. Or there could be a *didactic* aim, in which case, either Plato wants to present certain theories of his own and so makes Socrates' interlocutors less objectionable, or, in good faith, he believes that what they assent to is what the reasoning would lead them to think. Alternatively, he could have both dialectical *and* didactic aims (in addition to his political and literary aims – see pages xx and 28).

Either way, a change needs to be made to the classroom practice of this dialectical method. The change, however, is *directional* rather than substantive. If Plato's aim is *dialectical*, then the dialectic needs to be elicited from the group itself, rather than from any supposed observer to the discussion. This is probably the clearest difference between the literary dialogues and any imitation of Platonic dialogues in real life. And if his aim is *didactic*, again, that would have no place in a classroom engaged in pursuing dialectical philosophy together. In other words, there are certain literary devices employed by Plato that have no place in actual classroom practice, yet the dialectical devices he uses are modelled so that we may use them in actual classroom practice.

In practical terms, this means that the PhiE facilitator does not ask leading questions to the extent that Socrates does (and if s/he does then it is only of the *inferential* kind – see page 57 in Vol. 2), that s/he does not 'join in', or become a *participant* as Socrates does, and that s/he only performs a *structural role* ensuring that the content belongs to the participants. But these changes may in fact bring the classroom practice of Socratic dialogues more in line what I have described as Socrates' 'ideal practice', as described in his midwifery analogy in *Theaetetus* (see page 69), thereby freeing the pedagogy in Plato's dialogues from the dialectical and didactic rhetoric.

Finally, there are often attempts to make a case for doing philosophy on the basis that it provides instrumental benefits to those who do it. Increases in confidence (Murris 1992; Trickey 2007; Gorard et al. 2015; Siddiqui et al. 2017), decreases in psychotic tendencies (Colon et al. 2014), improved reasoning (Trickey & Topping 2004) and benefits to reading and maths performance (Gorard et al. 2015) are some of the beneficial outcomes of doing philosophy that you may read about.

My colleague, Andy West, worked with a boy (whom I will call 'David'), who was terminally ill, for whom there were to be no long-term benefits of doing philosophy. He loved doing philosophy and insisted on continuing with it to the very end of his life. In this story, there is both a confirmation and a challenge to Socrates who said, 'I am afraid that other people do not realise that the one aim of those who practice philosophy in the proper manner is to practice for dying and death' (*Phaedo* 64a). Perhaps there was a sense in which David was coping with his terminal situation by doing philosophy, but what my colleague and I drew from this was not his preparing for death but David's 'present' engagement in the precious little of life left to him. There are those who live much longer lives who fail to be as *present*.

NOTES

1. The term 'P4C' (Philosophy for Children) was first coined by Matthew Lipman to describe his approach and curriculum, also developed with Ann Margaret Sharp. 'PwC' (Philosophy with Children) was introduced later to describe 'offshoots' of Lipman's original approach and curriculum. 'P4/wC' is used to capture all these approaches, and which are all understood to be based on and indebted to the Lipman/ Sharp foundations. PhiE is perfectly compatible with other approaches to doing philosophy, especially when it comes to the dialectical questioning aspect. A questioning aspect features in all approaches to doing philosophy.

2. Here is a good presentation of the 10-step model of P4/wC: https://dialoguework s.co.uk/wp-content/uploads/2019/05/P4C-10-step-model.pdf.

3. See David Shapiro's account of similar difficulties implementing the IAPC curriculum in school in the United States in his introduction to his book *Plato Was Wrong!* (2012).

4. The editor of this series of books, Thomas Wartenberg, unbeknownst to me at that time, was developing a similar approach. See his book *Big Ideas for Little Kids* (Rowman & Littlefield 2009, 2014) where he also makes a case for departing from the Lipmanian tradition of P4C.

5. Hadot uses the word 'orient'.

Part One

Philosophy and Dialectic

WHAT IS PHILOSOPHY?[1]

Philosophy; *noun*, the study of the fundamental nature of knowledge, reality and existence. (Dictionary definition)

Given that we at The Philosophy Foundation train people how to conduct philosophical conversations, one of the first things we do on our preliminary PhiE training course is to ask the attendees what philosophy is, and then, in the context of what they say, we say something about how it is understood within PhiE.

To address what philosophy is, rather than try to answer the question of what philosophy is exhaustively – a notoriously difficult endeavour – I engage the attendees in a values-elicitation exercise. What I ask them to do is to imagine that they have been asked by a pupil, a teacher, parent or school secretary what philosophy is. Then I ask them to hone in on what they think is most important for a possible *short* answer, regarding what philosophy is more generally, but also how they think it will best relate to pupils, teachers or parents, and to others.

In his introduction to the book of the podcast series *Philosophy Bites* (2012), Nigel Warburton says, 'Philosophy is an unusual subject in that its practitioners don't agree what it's about'. In fact, many of the philosophers he asks this question come across as somewhat backfooted. Jeff McMahan says, somewhat ironically, 'Can I just laugh? I have no idea what philosophy is'.

What we get when we look at a survey of different philosopher's answers to this question is the values of the philosophers who answer it.[2] There are, however, certain concepts that emerge again and again: Maria Popova, in her summary of the *Philosophy Bites* introduction for her blog *Brain Pickings* (see footnote 2), helpfully identifies three main components that emerge from the numerous definitions given: *critical thinking, sensemaking*, and *presuppositions*.

I find this helpful and so I've chosen one quote that Popova associates with each of these categories that I might use (or adapt) to tell a pupil, a teacher, a parent or school secretary what it is I am about to start doing with their children (all from Eddings and Warburton 2012). Or, should I say, 'what it is I am about to get their children doing'? Follow the link at footnote 2 for more definitions of philosophy.

On philosophy as *critical thinking*:

> 'Philosophy is 99 percent about critical reflection on anything you care to be interested in'. (Richard Bradley)

On philosophy as *sensemaking*:

> 'Most simply put, it's about making sense of all this. . . . We find ourselves in a world that we haven't chosen. There are all sorts of possible ways of interpreting it and finding meaning in the world and in the lives that we live. So philosophy is about making sense of that situation that we find ourselves in'. (Clare Carlisle)

On philosophy as *presuppositions*:

> 'Philosophy has always been something of a science of presuppositions; but it shouldn't just expose them and say "there they are". It should say something further about them that can help people'. (Tony Coady)

But for a more general definition, the shortest best answer is often heard: that philosophy is *thinking about thinking*, but probably the best general answer is the one given by Wilfred Sellars in *Philosophy and the Scientific Image of Man*:

> 'The aim of philosophy, abstractly formulated, is to understand how things in the broadest possible sense of the term hang together in the broadest possible sense of the term. . . .To achieve success in philosophy would be, to use a contemporary turn of phrase, to "know one's way around"'. (Sellars 1962)[3]

Philosophy as Conversation

What is missing from all these – otherwise helpful – definitions is the role of *conversation* in philosophy and this is where we may turn to the Greeks, and particularly Socrates. Socrates not only put conversation at the heart of philosophy, believing that thinking is itself a kind of conversation that one has with oneself (see page 72 in Vol. 2), but he also had a unique way of utilising conversation.

Hadot says that '[Socrates'] philosophical method consists not in transmitting knowledge (which would mean responding to his disciples' questions) but in questioning his disciples'. This distinction is central to how PhiE approaches doing philosophy and how it sees itself following in the Socratic tradition. Nigel Warburton echoes Hadot (see pages xxx–xxxii) when he says in this article 'Talk with Me' (Aeon)[4] that it is conversation that distinguishes philosophy from dogma.

In the *Phaedrus* dialogue Plato has Socrates go one further when he has him say that true philosophy cannot be done well via the written word (a relatively new technology then), as written words cannot answer questions, clarify or qualify and there is no context for the words to be found within and measured against.

The irony is that this is said *in a book*. However, it is a book that, with many of Plato's other dialogues, imitates conversation. It is written in dialogue-form, containing discussions between two or more interlocutors. Many of the dialogues are also written to be open-ended, either discreetly, in that many of the dialogues literally end inconclusively (e.g., *Euthyphro* and *Meno*, to name but two) or continuously, in that the conclusions of one dialogue are challenged (or demolished) in others (e.g., *the theory of Forms* in *Republic* and *the third man argument* against this theory in *Parmenides*). This open-endedness invites more conversation.

Finally, Plato's dialogues imitate conversation in that they seem – more than to invite – to *invoke* the reader as an active, critical participant in that she evaluates the proceedings, synoptically, and though inevitably from something of a distance, she is invited to be part of the conversation. The reader of Platonic dialogues often finds herself 'shouting at the TV' – as it were – and this is just what Plato would have wanted us to do (see page 12 in Vol. 2). This is how he resolved the paradox, and how he, ingeniously, preserved the conversational aspect of doing philosophy, so dear to Socrates, while at the same time, through writing, preserved the words that, after a conversation had finished, would otherwise 'fall to the ground' (*Euthyphro* 14d) and be lost forever.

This 'conversational' model of doing philosophy is central to both a Platonic conception of doing philosophy and to PhiE. Hadot says that in antiquity 'philosophy and philosophical discourse thus appear to be simultaneously incommensurable and inseparable' (2004).

The 4 'R's

I have previously found it useful (Worley 2015b)[5] to describe the process of philosophising as having four components, captured by four 'R's. According to this model, doing philosophy is

- **Responsive** – this has three parts to it: there is the initial *intuitive responses* to the stimulus (whether this may be a classic philosophical text, a story or a picture book, etc.) and these responses can have many characters: philosophical, narrative, emotional, even procedural. The second kind of responsiveness is of a more philosophical character, when the participants start to see a problem or problems, a component of doing philosophy I call 'problem-seeing' (see pages 9 of Vol. 1 and 69 of Vol. 2). And, if one is doing philosophy in a group, one may also be responsive to others in the group, including to oneself (see pages xxviii, 2, 13 of Vol. 1 and 72 of Vol. 2).
- **Reflective** – this is where the participants, reader or students begin to ponder, to consider and to question (both, to *ask questions* and to put something *into question* – see pages 79–80 of Vol. 1 and 67 of Vol. 2). Reflection is where the state of mind of the participants is one of sensitivity to doubts, alternatives, possibilities and contingencies.
- **Reasoned** – this is the process of justifying, ordering and sequencing in thought through the use of critical, inferential, inductive and deductive moves. This aspect has persuasive force: it can bring someone to a particular view or change their mind about something.
- **Re-evaluative** – this is the point at which participants begin to re-think, re-consider or re-shape their initial intuitions, beliefs, arguments and conclusions in light of any reasoning and reflection done earlier by themselves or others. Moving into this mode of philosophising does not necessarily mean that one *does* or *should* change one's mind or shift one's thinking, it means that one should be open to doing this *should there be good reason to do so.*

Philosophy does not necessarily have to always happen in the order laid out above, but it should always involve these aspects. For PhiE, you are simply not doing philosophy if you are not, at some point, responding, reflecting, reasoning or re-evaluating. The four 'R's model of doing philosophy also corresponds with the basic model derived from the analysis of Heraclitus' dialectical effect (see pages 14–17).

Logos and Flux

Among the debates within the question of what philosophy is are whether philosophy is intuitive and emotional or rational, whether it is collaborative or oppositional, truth-seeking or sceptical, democratic or elitist, driving towards consensus or divergent, an enlightenment ideal or a postmodern deconstruction tool, analytic or hermeneutical and so on and so forth. To understand how one might begin to resolve these debates we need to turn away from Socrates and his search for exhaustive definitions and towards the pre-Socratic philosophers, in particular, Heraclitus, and the notion of the *unity of opposites* (see also page 36): the yin-yang-like notion *that something, in some way, both is and is not and that opposites share in one another.*

Often mistakenly credited – thanks to Plato – with inventing and advocating the *doctrine of flux* (that everything changes), Heraclitus offered a much more interesting – and helpful – idea: that everything changes *and* that things do not change. This seems both intuitively right, while at the same time appearing to be unthinkable, after all, (within classical logic) didn't Aristotle tell us that the *law of non-contradiction* is inviolable?

Thinking the unthinkable[6] becomes possible when one considers that in one sense of *change* it can be maintained that everything changes (i.e., the river flows) and in another, that things do not change (i.e., it has the same name and carries me from A to B again and again). Or, to put it another way: change can occur to *one and the same* thing (see Aristotle's account of how in his notion of *substances and properties*).

This Heraclitean paradox is at the heart of philosophy itself. Philosophy has two fundamentally dialectical aspects that remain locked in an eternal dance, neither able to *draw closer to* nor *pull away from* each other. These conceptual features can be captured in the Greek concepts of *logos* (reason/account from which we get our 'logic') and *flux* (change/flow). Here they are, as categories, together with the sorts of things done in philosophical practice that they capture as correspondences to one another (this is by no means an exhaustive list):

Logos	Flux
Seeking definitions	Seeking counterexamples to definitions
Making judgements	Re-evaluating judgements already made
Seeking consensus	Seeking controversy
Seeking consistency	Seeking inconsistency (tensions, contradictions, and paradoxes)
Seeking certainty	Scepticism
Providing reasons	Eliciting Intuitions
Agreeing	Disagreeing
Seeking generality/principles	Seeking particular examples
Disrupting order	Seeking order
Following sequence	Randomness
Stasis (is)	Dynamism (becoming)
Structure	Content
Interpretation	Re-interpretation
Singular	Multiple
Scholastic (theoretical)	Of the world
Apollonian (see below)	Dionysian (see below)

Philosophy is, therefore, the negotiation of both *logos* and *flux* in consideration of and in attempts to understand and articulate thoughts and ideas about ourselves, the world and each other. This 'Heraclitean' definition of philosophy resolves many of the perennial arguments about which side of the coin philosophy falls, whether it is analytic or continental, rational or intuitive and so on. The answer is always, 'both'. Pierre Hadot (2002) encapsulates what philosophy is in these words:

> The practice of philosophy transcends the oppositions of particular philosophies.[7] It is essentially an effort to become aware of ourselves, our being in the world, and our becoming with others. It is also, as Maurice Merleau-Ponty used to say, an effort to 'relearn how to see the world' and attain a universal vision, thanks to which we can put ourselves in the place of others and transcend our own partiality. (p. 276)

A further feature of philosophy that is curiously missing from the dictionary definition (see page 1) is that it is also an *activity*. One can learn about the *history of ideas* and sit tests on how much one has managed to remember, but to be a *philosopher*, rather than a 'student of the history of ideas', one needs to regularly engage in *philosophising*, or in the *doing* of philosophy. Though PhiE does not ignore the history of ideas (see page 87 of Vol. 2), in line with Socrates, its emphasis is very much on the activity of doing philosophy, and doing so with others (see pages 26 and 37).

Ambivalence: Two-Eyed Thinking

Apropos the last line of Hadot's conception of philosophy as seeking to attain a 'universal vision' and 'transcending partiality', the writer Mark O'Connell, begins his Radio 4 programme 'The Courage of Ambivalence' (see Bibliography[8]) by drawing upon James Joyce's *Ulysses*, a story woven around Homer's *Odyssey*. He describes the encounter in the 'Cyclops' section of the book – where Leopold Bloom, one of the book's central characters, argues with someone known only as 'the Citizen' – as a metaphor for different ways of apprehending the world. The Citizen is, as O'Connell says, 'a metaphorically one-eyed character, capable of taking only one view on any issue. Bloom, on the other hand, is gloriously ambivalent, and in this sense, a kind of ideal, modern, democratic human'.

So, by ambivalence O'Connell is not talking about the everyday sense of the word where we might mean someone's being uninterested, un-invested or unconcerned, he is talking about *being able to hold more than one position on an issue simultaneously, to see more than one side*, and perhaps also *to hold onto contradictory positions*.

PhiE is an approach to doing philosophy that, short of promoting wholesale ambivalence, allows for and lends itself to the cultivation of taking – and perhaps holding onto – different points of view. As O'Connell says, '. . . this conflict feels very relevant to where we are today, people seem more divided than ever'. He concludes this thought with, 'There are more "Citizens" around and fewer "Blooms"'. A participant may well begin a PhiE seeing only one position, but the process requires that they apply proper consideration (see page 28 in Vol. 2) to the issues, and this is done, procedurally, by sitting with others and listening openly to their points of view, beliefs and positions.

It is very difficult to do this without, to some extent anyway, *opening both eyes*.[9] The hope is that this eventually results in a process of internalisation where the different perspectives and points of view begin to occur in the mind of one person when they stop to consider something , not merely when they stop to listen to others. One of the main aims of doing philosophy in PhiE is to encourage 'Two-eyed thinking' even where, at the end, a singular judgement is made (see 'Silent dialogue' on page 72 of Vol. 2 and 'The paradox of Socrates' on page 42).

The Reason for Reason in Philosophy

There are legitimate worries about the role of reason and rationality throughout the history of ideas particularly when understood as instruments of immoral ends, such as racism, anti-Semitism, human and intellectual purges and other crimes against humanity, and given philosophy's close association with reason, this worry may transpose to philosophy too.

It is worth noting that many have levelled this charge at Plato, particularly for the proposals he is seen to make in *Republic*; we should, however, remember that it was written as a dialogue, not a treatise (Higgins 2008). Nevertheless, one should carefully distinguish between *reason* and the *uses and abuses of reason*.

When we spot a questionable use of reason to promote racial hierarchy, for instance, the best tool to which we can appeal to counter it is reason itself (see, for instance, *How to Argue with a Racist* by Adam Rutherford [2020]). To do so, we may look for contradictions or inconsistencies, for example. It is here that we reach the paradox of arguments against reason: any arguments against reason must appeal to reason in some way, and if one avoids reason, one is open to the charge of being unwarranted.

PhiE does not appeal to any ideology premised on convoluted strings of contestable reasoning, as arguments for white supremacy or the inferiority of women might; it merely appeals to the basic mechanisms of thought, basic inferences and the structure of reason-giving, or justification (see page xxviii), and reason is free of the charge of immorality because, as with a good knife, it cannot be put on trial itself, only those who wield it.

Developing good, *intellectual virtues* can help one use the tool(s) of reason well. Here is a condensed starting-list of intellectual virtues based on achieving rational ends:

> We understand critical thinking to be purposeful, self-regulatory judgment which results in interpretation, analysis, evaluation, and inference, as well as explanation of the evidential, conceptual, methodological, criteriological, or contextual considerations upon which that judgment is based. . . . The ideal critical thinking is habitually inquisitive, well-informed, trustful of reason, open-minded, flexible, fair-minded in evaluation, honest in facing personal biases, prudent in making judgments, willing to reconsider, clear about issues, orderly in complex matters, diligent in seeking relevant information, reasonable in the selection of criteria, focused in inquiry, and persistent in seeking results which are as precise as the subject and the circumstances of inquiry permit. (Facione, 1989)[10]

Another worry regarding reason is that *dialectical philosophy* could be thought to impose logic and reasoning onto those engaged in doing PhiE, forcing participants into logical binaries and therefore into conclusions based on binaries. The ancient Greeks are often seen as the progenitors of the rational project; sometimes Athens (the Acropolis in particular) is seen as the *throne of European rationality*, and – so the thought goes – as the rational, imperial *sovereign of the world*. But this is to misunderstand both reason and, especially, the Greek approach to it. The Greeks were as paradoxical as the rest of us.

As well as developing systematic rational ways of looking at the world, such as history, mathematics, philosophy, science and so on (systems often begun by earlier civilisations), the Greeks also held many beliefs and pursued many practices that stand in contradiction to the rational project: ceremonies, superstitions, rituals and narratives that embraced the non-rational, the irrational, the mystical and the ineffable.

These two distinct sides to Greek culture are nicely captured in the concepts surrounding the gods *Apollo* and *Dionysus* (Nietzsche 1999). Apollo, the sun god, was the god of logic and order, symmetry, proportion, appealing to rationality, prudence and purity, while Dionysus was the god of wine, dance and intoxication, irrationality and chaos, appealing to emotions and instincts. The Greeks were not one *or* the other, Socrates was not one *or* the other (see 'The paradox of Socrates' on page 42): they were *both*. PhiE appeals to Socrates (through Plato and Aristotle) for the method, but it also appeals to Heraclitus for the notion of *the unity of opposites* (see pages 4–5).

As well as appealing to both the rational and the intuitive (see page 6), and although the basic mechanism of PhiE (see page 3 of Vol. 2), being dialectical, is logic-based, the logic can be used to argue for A *or* not-A, or it can be used to make a case for A *and* not-A (children often do: 'I think yes *and* no', 'I think it *kind of* is and *kind of* isn't'). This may simply be a case of needing to draw some carefully wrought distinctions, but, where a case or point of consideration is subtler, more nuanced and more ephemeral, where simply applying the drawing of distinctions is not enough, or where the thinkers don't have subtle enough distinctions in place, PhiE still allows for expression of those thoughts.

Plato and Aristotle's own interpretations of Heraclitus misunderstood Heraclitus's expression in precisely this way: they claimed, what consequently most people think today, that Heraclitus thought *you cannot step into the same river twice,* quantising to the nearest reasonable side of the binary. But, what Heraclitus really thought was, embracing both sides of the binary, that *you can and you cannot* step into the same river twice (McCabe 1988, 2015). One may argue that this is nothing more than a difference of expression, but, it is a difference that allows for so much more, for a position of *ambivalence* (see above). Perhaps, Heraclitus saw with two eyes what Plato and Aristotle looked on with only one. So, if Plato and Aristotle embody, to some extent, the restrictive parochialism of rationality in this example, Heraclitus represents something much more synoptic and freeing.

Philo-Sophia and the Love of Learning

Education can be split into two aspects: *productivity* and *personal development.* It is cynical to think that education only pertains to the former, but it is naive to think it is only about the latter, and it certainly doesn't have to be one *or* the other. Many will be familiar with the roots of the word *philosophy* deriving from the ancient Greek words for 'love' (*philia*) and 'wisdom' (*sophia*) and usually interpreted together as 'love of wisdom'. The word 'school' also has its roots in the ancient world deriving from the Greek *skhole* (leisure, free time) that brings together the notions of 'leisure', 'philosophy' and 'lecture place'.

Interestingly, when doing PhiE, all three of these concepts are present: the activity is treated as something to be enjoyed (see page 37), and it makes use of the space and place in which it is done: the tables are moved, the chairs set up in a particular way to create a clear, physical 'space to think', distinguishing it from other lessons (see page xxiii in Vol. 2). And, finally, in Plato's *Meno* dialogue, Socrates suggests that learning itself is 'recollection' (*anamnesis*) of what is already present within the soul. These historical precedents all come together in the somewhat sentimental idea that school and education should engender a *love of learning.* But there is something important behind this idea and it brings together *desire* and *learning,* something that can be articulated via the ideas of Plato and Socrates.

In the *Symposium*, Plato's dialogue on Love (*Eros*), Diotima, who is teaching Socrates about Love, is asked by Socrates, '. . . who *are* the people who love wisdom, if they are neither wise nor ignorant?' to which she replies, 'That's obvious [. . .] a child could tell you'. And, indeed, the answer lies in what it is to be a child, described in what Diotima goes on to say next: '. . . those who love wisdom fall *in between* those two extremes' (*Symposium* 204b). But what we notice when we step back a little more is that this is the case for all humans. In this way, *we are all children.*

For Plato, love (or desire) motivates one towards wisdom and knowledge because we do not possess them but we apprehend them well enough to know that we want them and that they are worth attaining. So, learning and wisdom are to this extent *erotic*. But given how people today understand this word, I should qualify: they are *erotic* in that they *yearn for that which is lacked but that we should have and so desire*. If we think of ourselves as philosophers (literally, '*lovers* of wisdom'), though we can, perhaps, 'never attain wisdom, [we] can make progress in its direction' (Hadot 2002).

The value of philosophical enquiry may be framed as whether or not one has answered a 'big question', but whether or not the big question is answered, much can be gained along the way, for instance, answering smaller questions, understanding others better and being better understood.

In his book, *Shakespeare's Philosophy* (2006), Colin McGinn quotes Aristotle's *Metaphysics*: 'All men naturally desire knowledge'. McGinn goes on to say, 'The skeptic is a kind of tragedian about knowledge: he admits that Aristotle's dictum is correct but he claims that this desire is necessarily thwarted'. Short of denying *all and any* claims to knowledge, in its fullest sense, knowledge is always denied us; there is always more to know, and there are holes and gaps in what we do know, there are constant revisions to what we think we know and, very likely, insurmountable limits to what we can ever know, from our singular human perspective.

The upside to all this is that it is precisely this aspect of the human condition that has the effect of motivating, or instilling and triggering the desire for knowledge Aristotle spoke of. When children realise that they don't know something or recognise that they are faced with a problem, most are, when the conditions are right (see page 57), spurred into action and thought. So, when I see a group of children suddenly recognise that they are faced with a philosophical problem, such as whether or not you can step into the same river twice, what I see is a healthy, human response to employ their reason to resolve it and to reach out for that which they do not have (this is the nature of *Eros* in *Symposium*). Sometimes, *some* resolution *is* achieved, if not regarding the ends that are sought, at least regarding clarifications of thought along the way.

It is the fact that children are in possession of concepts and language to apprehend and articulate them that makes doing philosophy possible with children. Yet it is also the vagueness of those concepts and the gaps in their knowledge that makes philosophy immediate, something they *just do* and *step into* under the right conditions, with very little coaxing. In this sense, and with qualifications (see page 56), children make very natural philosophers. But, as well as being that which propels children to do philosophy, I would argue that it is, perhaps among other things, this 'epistemological tragedy' that makes philosophy urgent for us all.

Desire and knowledge and wisdom are intrinsically linked, as Socrates and Plato suggest, and when they are piqued in the right way and at the right time, what follows is what can be described as the psychological, the intellectual and social conditions for the stirrings of a 'love of learning', about wisdom and knowledge and how they are related.

Part of what it is to mature intellectually (also see page 53) is to realise that there are limits to knowledge but it is also to make one's way to the borders of thought and knowledge, to discover for oneself what and where those limits are, how they are drawn, and perhaps to redraw them oneself.

And to the Children?

If the children ask 'What is philosophy?', I always begin by saying to the class that philosophy is 'to do with thinking' (when I introduce them to the Dialectical Triangle, this expands to 'thinking, speaking and listening' – see page 2 of Vol. 2). Philosophy is therefore something they can do, even if they can't *say* it correctly. Later, I may add that it is about 'saying what you think and why you think it', and 'saying what you think about what others think and why you think it' (see page 3 of Vol. 2). Crucially, it is about *deciding for yourself what you think the best answer to a question is, based on the best reasons you can think of or have heard* (this becomes easier when they start learning about the criteria for deciding what make for good reasons – see page 98 in Vol. 2). And, finally, I'll add that *it's okay to change your mind about stuff!*

A Word about Right and Wrong Answers in Philosophy

It is often said, by children, parents and teachers that *there are no right and wrong answers in philosophy*. Although it is understandable why people may say this, it is not true. One of the assumptions about philosophy that underpins PhiE is that one of the main aims of a philosophical conversation is that participants are engaged on a collective attempt to work *towards* a right answer, or 'the most reasonable answer' (Reznitskaya & Wilkinson 2017).

And in philosophy, the best answers in respect of candidacy to being true, acceptable, possible or morally right are the best in virtue of the quality of the reasoning behind them and how the reasoning accords with or challenges our intuitions. That notion of *towards* does not mean that the most reasonable answer is always or automatically correct or true (etc.), and it is this sensitivity that makes all answers in philosophy therefore *provisional*: they remain – however good – open to *revision* or *rejection*.

This *provisionality* is, in the best examples, what most people mean when they say that 'there are no right and wrong answers in philosophy'. But, however well-intentioned, it remains an inaccurate and misleading phrase. Expanding on what I've recommended you say to the children about what philosophy is above, here is something that you could say to the children (depending on their age), and, even if you don't say this all at once, you could say it over time, or have it written up on the classroom wall, either as written below or as bullet points (see also page 65):

Philosophy is about using your minds, by thinking, speaking and listening, to consider what is possible and impossible, what is right and wrong, what is true and false, and what makes sense or doesn't, while trying your best to *understand* and properly *consider* the ideas of others in the group. It is also important to make yourself as *clear* as possible so that others may understand you. Philosophy is about saying *what you think in answer to questions* and *giving reasons* for what you think, and there may or may not be a right or wrong answer at any one time in philosophy; it is for *you to decide for yourself* whether you think there is a right or wrong answer *based on the best reasons* you can think of or have heard. You can change your mind *if you think there are good reasons to do so.* You can *disagree* with what others (or yourself) have said, so long as you disagree *respectfully* and give *reasons for why you disagree.*

DIALECTIC

This section explains, in some detail, what is meant by this somewhat intimidating word and shows what role dialectic plays in PhiE and how its role has been drawn from the Greeks who approached philosophy dialectically, and what's more, systematically so. This section is important because of the centrality of some key aspects of the practice of PhiE that come directly from this discussion: namely, the best kind of 'question' for use in PhiE (the 'Heraclitean' grammatically closed but conceptually open question), the basic mechanism and movement within a PhiE (as represented by the 'Parmenidean' dialectical triangle – see page 2 of Vol. 2) and the central questioning technique (the 'Platonic' if-ing, anchoring and opening-up questioning strategy), and the 'Aristotelean/Heraclitean' stages of a PhiE's development. If Heraclitus puts the world into a shimmering flux of contingent possibilities, if he transforms the world into *questions* rather than a fixed, static entity that we simply bump into (Bowker 2010), then Parmenides provides us with the beginnings of a systematic tool for us to start answering the question, namely: *dialectic.*

The Origins of Dialectic

In his two-pronged *Proem*[11] 'The way of truth and the way of belief', Parmenides outlines what McCabe (1982, 2015) calls the 'rules of dialectic': McCabe's formulation of his assumption is that '. . . you can think and you can speak'. The 'you' implies that there must be more than one so that it is a *thinking and speaking exchange.* This can be literal, between two or more people, or it can be figurative: speaking with oneself *as if* there is more than one person (see page 72 in Vol. 2). Another way of understanding the dialectical relationship is that between the reader and the text (see pages xxxiii, 3, 23, 64 and 77) where the text 'says' something to which the reader responds: 'I agree', 'I disagree', 'I don't understand', etc.

One of Parmenides' innovations was to show that reason can be employed, through the medium of language, and structured according to logic, to persuade and make a case. Even earlier, Heraclitus showed how a question can instigate a *dialectical effect* (see page 15), implying the back-and-forth movement and ensuing argumentation that by Parmenides' time had become explicit. This was the origin of the intellectual processes that would enable the Greeks to develop a systematic method of rational thought making truth-seeking an open-access domain, for anyone capable of thought, not merely, as had been before, the preserve of a priest-class or an authoritarian fiat. More than democracy, this rational discourse is possibly the greatest gift the Greeks gave the world.

Socrates built on these two foundations to develop a highly sophisticated use of sustained question-and-answer exchanges to consider and investigate – in Socrates' case, *philosophical* – opinions. Plato, in turn, built on this to develop and show us a dialectical method for conducting philosophy that laid the foundations for later historical developments such as the scientific method itself. Aristotle built on what his predecessors had done, making – being more wisely tentative – dialectic a medium for understanding, rather than for giving access to robust knowledge as Plato had hoped it would. Although Aristotle moved away from the overt conversational style Socrates had given birth to, he always remained locked in a dialectical relationship with Plato (McCabe 2015) implying an ongoing 'conversation' between them.

Because of its approachability, it is the Socratic question-and-answer talk that roots PhiE (and probably all other ways of doing philosophy with children and in other settings, or the *agora* – see pages xx and xxx) in ancient Greek culture. Throughout this book, the word *dialectic* (which literally means 'through speech') will be used to describe this question-and-answer talk that is the starting place for doing philosophy with children.

To be a little more precise, by *dialectic* I mean *the systematic investigation, exploration and evaluation of opinions around a question by means of sequential, question-and-answer conversations.* McCabe (1982, 2015) says,

> By dialectic, I mean to suggest two conditions: (a) that the process of discourse be carried on by more than one person. There is a questioner and a respondent. The latter may only listen; but nevertheless, dialectic supposes a more-or-less attentive audience. This condition is independent of but probably generates (b) that the philosophical outcome is tentative. Its success depends not on 'getting the right answer', but on the exploratory process itself. Hence Aristotle's description of dialectic as *peirastike*, the art of trying and testing; Metaphysics 1004b25.[12]

(See pages 13, 22 and 24 for more on differences between Platonic and Aristotelean dialectic.)

Heraclitus

Heraclitus (c. 535–475 BCE) was a Pre-Socratic philosopher from Ephesus, a Greek colony on the coast of Asia Minor (modern Turkey). Hall (2015) has suggested that one reason he may have asked questions about changing rivers is because of the ever-changing coast around Miletus (another intellectual centre of ancient Greece) and Ephesus; he would have witnessed very visible changes to the coastline every year.

Although the preferred question-type for PhiE had been arrived at long before I found this correspondence in Heraclitus, McCabe's analysis and subsequent insights are of such importance to understanding PhiE that I have decided to make this historical correspondence central to the presentation of the theory behind PhiE.

As you can see on pages 14–15 in Vol. 2, the preferred question-type for a PhiE is a *grammatically closed* yet *conceptually open* question. One of the best examples of this question-type, 'Can you step into the same river twice?', can be sourced to Heraclitus, though it does not appear in any of the historical fragments in this particular 'question formulation'. The three fragments that do exist, however, allow us to see how this question-type works, why PhiE prefers it and how PhiE follows this model, thanks to insights afforded by McCabe (1988, 2015).

The Dialectical Effect: Thinking Flows like a River

A question of this type triggers what McCabe calls *the dialectical effect*. When one asks the question 'Can you step into the same river twice?' the first psychological move is to answer in a way that is most intuitive: perhaps, with this example, 'Yes, of course: you step in, then step out, then step in again'. This can be described as what McCabe calls the *doxa* from the Greek, meaning 'opinion' or 'belief'. Yet the accompanying thought to this is almost one of distain: 'But this is so obvious why would you ask that question in the first place?' This is how many people – children and adults – will likely start in answer to this question.

This triggers two possible responses: first, it implies the opposite of the intuitive response, that perhaps the questioner thinks, 'You cannot step into the same river twice', which leads very quickly to 'why?'; but if not this, it triggers, even if only momentarily, a *search*: 'What possible reason could someone have for thinking that you can't step into the same river twice?' Either of these two threads lead to: 'You cannot step into the same river twice because the waters that make up the river flow and are therefore always changing'. Which leads to a paradox: 'But now it seems that the river is the same river [see the obvious intuitive response above], but also that it is not the same river [for the reasons just given]'.

The problem is: 'it can't both be the same river and a different river, can it?' By enquiring into this it could lead to a solution: 'It can [both be the same river and a different river] if we understand there to be more than one kind of *same* and/or more than one kind of sense of *river*'.

Here's the problem behind Heraclitus' question in a nutshell. Philosophers distinguish between *numerical* identity (made of the very same, countable things) and *qualitative* identity (sharing properties). Two things are numerically identical when they are the very same object ('That's the exact same pencil I had this morning!'); two things are qualitatively identical when they are the same kind of object ('The Nile and the Thames are the same in that they are both rivers').

The problem raised by Heraclitus' question is when we try to say that something is the same (numerically identical) even though it has changed in some way. It seems intuitive to say that when we swim in a river for the second time it is the same river but it is also intuitive to say that its physical composition is different (some of the water will have evaporated, some of it will have flowed into the sea, etc.) The philosophical question philosophers are interested in, and

have been since Heraclitus, may be put as follows: can we (and if so how?) say
that something that has undergone change over time remains the same thing?

Finally, the question invites any contemplators to generalise from the particular: 'Perhaps this is not about rivers so much as *change* in general: can
anything be the same thing if it changes through time?' These stages of *the
dialectical effect* are tracked if we place Heraclitus' fragments alongside one
another as McCabe does (1988, 2015) like so:

- Can you step into the same river twice? (Question formulation implied by
  fragments, *grammatically closed but conceptually open* – see pages 14–15
  in Vol. 2)
- Yes: you step in, step out, then step in again. (*Doxa*: intuitive, pre-reflective
  response to the question)
- [Fragment] It is impossible to step into the same river twice. (Alternative,
  antithetical view that accompanies the intuitive response to the question)
- [Fragment] We both step and do not step, are and are not in the same rivers.
  (The paradox)
- [Fragment] To those who step into the same rivers, ever different waters
  flow. (Possible solution: to separate out and distinguish between different
  concepts of *same* and possibly also *river*)
- [Fragment][13] The universe flows like a river. (From the particular: *rivers*, to
  the general: *change*)

As if to confirm the power of the dialectical effect, in a very short stream of
consciousness in Joyce's *Ulysses*, the character Leopold Bloom, while very
briefly reflecting on Heraclitus' question, also starts with the identity of rivers
and ends with a general insight about life itself:

> 'Good idea that. Wonder if he pays rent to the corporation. How can you own
> water really? It's always flowing in a stream, never the same, which in the
> stream of life we trace. Because life is a stream'. (Joyce, Ulysses, 1922 [2010],
> p. 136)

And although the order is not always the same, these stages chart how conversations around this question generally go in classrooms. One 10/11-year-old boy
once said in answer to a question of this nature: 'There's two answers to this:
there's the obvious answer and there's the philosophical answer'. (Heraclitus's,
Plato's and Aristotle's dialectical method – see below – in a nutshell!).

See page 125 in Vol. 2 for a lesson plan structured around the psychological progress mapped out by McCabe and based on classroom practice that
confirms this analysis in how the children's progress matches it more-or-less.

Sometimes they come to the fragments in a slightly different order and sometimes they cover only some of the stages.

Here are some questions that exemplify good questions for PhiE, all of which trigger the Heraclitean *dialectical effect* and all of which are grammatically closed yet conceptually open (see pages 14–15 of Vol. 2): 'Are we travelling through time?' (Worley 2015b), 'Is there a thought in this sentence?' (ibid.), 'Where is a piece of music?' (see page 122 in Vol. 2), 'Are we free?' (Worley 2012), or 'Can a smartphone think?' (Worley 2015b).

While reading these questions, you will probably have experienced *the dialectical effect* within yourself, perhaps thinking something like, 'Well *in a way* yes and *in a way* no . . .' or 'It depends what you mean by . . .' and so on; thoughts that, when the question is given some time and proper consideration, should begin to *flow like a river!* If you did, then it demonstrates, directly to the reader, the effectiveness of this technique and that what is needed, for you to be able to proceed with or *into* a philosophical discussion, is – as Socrates tells us (see below) – *within yourself* (see page 70).

Importantly, where you, or *any* single person, may have stopped moving deeper dialectically, someone else could take over (see page 62). This is the value of group work when engaging in dialectical philosophy.

The PhiE dialectical model, then, corresponding to this analysis, is as follows:

- Question
- Initial response(s) (intuitive or alternative)
- Search for alternatives (if necessary)
- Emergence of paradox(es) or problem(s)
- Attempts to resolve paradox(es) or problem(s)
- Continual navigation between the concrete and abstract (see 'The Hokey Kokey Method' on page 76 in Vol. 2)

Socrates

It is far from clear that there is a single Socratic dialectical method, but 'outlines' of methods in the dialogues themselves are discernible. Probably the most well-known method that has been attributed to Socrates is what has become known as the *elenchus*. This word is usually translated as 'refutation' but this suggests that Socrates' project was determinedly negative. Putting to one side any distinction there may be between the historical and the Platonic Socrates (see page xix), it is not always the case that Socrates' project is negative, sometimes he is arguing for positive theses such as that no one does wrong willingly, that virtue is knowledge, that virtue is sufficient for happiness and that no one desires to do evil.

McCabe has suggested that *elenchus* translates better as 'investigation' (2015),[14] and I will go with this translation choice. Whether you agree that there is a single unified method throughout *at least* the 'Socratic dialogues' (those earlier dialogues thought to be Plato's attempt to paint a portrait of the historical figure – see pages xix–xx) there *are* instances of a discernible method that moves, systematically, between the abstract and the concrete (see Hokey Kokey on page 76 in Vol. 2 for how this can be applied in classrooms) around a question of the form 'What is X?'. This *elenchus* can be described in the following terms and it can also be witnessed in the *Euthyphro*[15] dialogue (see page 102 of Vol. 2 for a classroom exercise based on this):

1. A *concept* is made salient during conversation and a question is asked apropos the concept under consideration (in the case of the *Euthyphro*, the concept is *piety*), 'What is X?' (*Euthyphro* 5d)
2. A *starting definition* is offered, usually by Socrates' interlocutor in response to the question. (Ibid. 7a)
3. The definition is *examined* and *difficulties* are uncovered, usually a *counterexample* is offered or an *inconsistency* (leading to a *contradiction*) is identified between two or more already held beliefs or statements that *refutes* (hence the usual translation of *elenchus* as 'refutation') the starting definition. (Ibid. 7a–9b)
4. A *general definition* is sought that would *accommodate all cases*. One might call this 'Socrates' definitional agenda'. (Ibid. 6d–e)
5. The starting definition is *amended* to *account for any difficulties*. (Ibid. 9e, 12e, 14d)
6. The process is repeated until a *satisfactory definition* is found or until the interlocutors depart. (Ibid. 9e–16a)

This process usually begins in the *concrete*: in a discussion to do with a particular real-life situation involving particular personages. For instance, in the *Euthyphro*, it begins in a discussion outside the courts where Socrates meets with him just as Euthyphro is about to prosecute this father for manslaughter. This brings the two of them to a discussion about piety (or 'godliness' or 'acting in accordance with the god's wishes') because it might be considered impious not to hold someone accountable for an injustice, but – perhaps more so in ancient Greek times than today – it was also considered impious to prosecute one's own father, even where an injustice had been committed.

Given 'Socrates' definitional agenda' (see 4 above), the discussion inevitably moves towards the abstract as Socrates explicitly forbids particular examples: he says, 'Bear in mind then that I did not bid you tell me one or two of the many pious actions . . .' then explains how they should seek '. . . that form itself that makes all X (pious) actions X (pious)'[16] (ibid. 6d–e). The word 'form' is *idea* in Greek. It is not clear at this stage whether this refers to the famous Platonic theory of Forms (with a capital 'F') or whether he just means something like 'notion'. In either case, he is asking for something general and abstract.

One worry about subscribing to a Socratic approach or to using a method like the *elenchus* is that it commits the participants to *essentialism*, the view that there is a stable, essential core at a concept's centre, one or more conceptual features that guarantee its instantiation; what is sought during an *elenctic* enquiry. Wittgenstein is well-known to have shown the problems with essentialism in his own idea of *family resemblances*: the claim that there need be no property that all individuals in a group share but a series of shifting resemblances. With this, Wittgenstein (2009) showed, quite intuitively, that families of things (*games* being his favourite example) do not necessarily have any one essential feature at their core.

Although Socrates was an *essentialist* (many Greeks were), his method of *elenchus* as a method is not committed to essentialism because, even though we may never find an essential list to a particular concept such as *art*, *rivers*, *truth*, *beauty*, or *philosophy* there is still value in examining these and other concepts because we may come to a more nuanced, richer concept than we started with. In other words, it is *improving* if not *exhaustive*. This can be easily seen with a classroom discussion where the class may start with a definition of a *lie* such as, 'When you say something wrong', but, having followed an elenchus-like process, end with, 'When you deliberately say something not true in order to mislead'.

Though there may be more counterexamples to come, the second is a much richer attempt at a definition. This *improving* aspect of the elenchus shows how the process, though seeming to be negative, may have a positive outcome.

Plato

Here is a paraphrase of Plato's own account of the journey through dialectic: it allows participants to grasp accounts of the being of things, to distinguish ideas in accounts by marking them off from everything else to have one's thoughts put through tests and to see if they survive those tests, testing according to how things are rather than according to opinion; to see if one's ideas can progress through all these things without one's account collapsing (Compare Plato's proposed progress with 'Answering PhiE Questions' in Vol. 2 on page 18) (*Republic 534b–c*).

As with Socratic dialectic, scholars do not agree about what exactly Platonic dialectic is, but many do agree that there is not one single method throughout the dialogues. Robinson (1953) said that the earlier dialogues concern themselves with *method* (how to do something) but not *methodology* (thinking about the method for how one does something), and the later dialogues with *methodology* but not *method*.

Very much in a Socratic spirit, Benson (2009) suggests that there is always an essential core that he says can be reduced to *two processes*: 'a process of identifying and drawing out the consequences of propositions, known as hypotheses, in order to answer the question at hand, and a process of confirming or justifying those hypotheses'. These methods can be captured in two structures: *hypothesis*: 'if . . . then . . .' and *justification*: 'x is/may be the case because . . .'. Benson goes on to say, 'The methods of *hypothesis* introduced in the *Meno* and again in the *Phaedo* and the method of *dialectic* explicitly introduced in the *Republic* are versions of a single core method' (ibid.).

Hypothesis and *justification* are also core to PhiE (see *if-ing, anchoring and opening-up* on page 41 of Vol. 2) and show a strong link between PhiE and Plato without having to be committed to Platonic metaphysics and epistemology. Benson also goes on to say, '. . . we should look at both Socrates' explicit discussions of method and his actual practice to understand dialectic' (ibid.). This book accords with this recommendation.

Just as Socrates' *elenchus* does not need a commitment to *essentialism* for it to be useful as a pedagogical, dialectical tool, neither does Platonic dialectic need a commitment to Platonic metaphysics and epistemology. After all, one might think that the methods employed by Socrates and his interlocutors, while they explore and argue for and against theories such as the Forms, remain distinct from such theories: the method may stand while the theory falls; in fact, the method may be the tool used to show that the theory stands or falls.

Aspects of Platonic Dialectic

McCabe (2006/15) provides a clear and insightful analysis of the structure of Platonic dialectic, the aspects of which have correspondence in PhiE and have directly informed its development. For McCabe (ibid.), dialectic has the following aspects (here, I quote McCabe at length):

1. a *logical* aspect: that the question and the answer represent two sides of a case, and the imagined conversation takes place as the two points of view play off against each other. This play has a compulsive side: these kinds of opposition demand resolution.
2. a *psychological* aspect: the philosopher remains agnostic, suspends judgement about which side of the case he proposes to take while he considers the matter; his agnostic stance is a sense of puzzlement, of aporia, in his soul, and the considering as something he does in his soul: e.g., at 524e5.

3. a *sequential* aspect: conversations are conducted in such a way that the answer is relevant to the question, and the next question to that answer. The notion of a conversation, that is, has an order, a proper sequence built in (compare Socrates' repeated insistence on doing things in the right order, e.g., at 527b, 528d, 535a).

4. An *epistemological* aspect: the philosopher takes a synoptic view of both sides of the case at once: he both entertains the opposed views and considers their relative merits. The synoptic view, that is, is reflective or second order; and it has both sides of the conversation within its scope (this is exemplified by Socrates' own reflective procedures, for example, at 529a-b; and see the ringing claim at 537c, that the dialectician is someone with a synoptic view).

5. *normativity*: you can do this kind of conversation well or badly; or fail to do it at all (see e.g., 525d, 527d, 528a, 531e-532a, 538–9).

Correspondence to PhiE

1. (*logical*) can be seen in PhiE by the use of grammatically closed but conceptually open questions (see pages 14–15 of Vol. 2) to instantiate a dialectical effect (see page 15); in the facilitator-technique of eliciting different sides of the 'dialectical coin' (see page 26 of Vol. 1, 'Thumb poll', 'Facilitating for dialectical movement' and 'The Response Detector and the Third Way' on pages 65, 5, and 62 of Vol. 2), and in the metacognitive techniques used to help the pupils strategise their attempts at resolution (see page 94 in Vol. 2).

2. (*psychological*) is seen in the *interest* and *willingness* that must be present in at least some of the group members at the start to trigger a dialectical effect in the group as a whole (see pages 55 and 9); in the growing sense of puzzlement that develops (see 'Aporia' on page 26 of Vol. 1 and page 38 of Vol. 2); in the motivation to resolve any problems (see page 9), and in the suspension of judgement the group is encouraged to take as it considers different ideas and perspectives before making judgements (see 'Truth and Knowlege' on page 63).

3. (*sequential*) can be seen particularly in the *opening-up* strategies (see pages 23 and 41 of Vol. 2); the use of *response detectors* (see page 62 of Vol. 2), *if-ing* and *anchoring* techniques (see pages 52 and 55 of Vol. 2); *emergent question* techniques (see page 66 of Vol. 2), and in how the facilitator and the group should listen in PhiE (see page 27 of Vol. 2).

4. (*epistemological*) can be seen in, among others, the *imaginary disagreer* move (see page 74 of Vol. 2); in the presence of 'Mappers' (see page 83 of Vol. 2); in the use of metacognitive questions: e.g., 'Have we answered the question?', 'Have we made good use of F's strategy of

finding counterexamples?' and so on (see 'Meta Task Question' on page 97 of Vol. 2); in linking moves and tension-play (see pages 62–65 of Vol. 2), and in PIES questions (see page 84 of Vol. 2).

5. (*normative*) can be seen in the metacognitive techniques for evaluating progress in a PhiE (see pages 84 and 97 of Vol. 2); the dialectical facilitation moves; the facilitator's own reflective evaluation of the enquiry , and in the teaching of the critical thinking tools that provide the criteria for evaluating better and worse arguments and ideas (see page 98 of Vol. 2).

Two Dialectics in Plato's Parmenides

In Plato's *Parmenides* dialogue, featuring a young Socrates and an older Parmenides, after Parmenides has devastated Socrates' beloved theory of Forms, Parmenides does a surprising thing. Rather than do a victory dance, he admits that the Forms are needed to save dialectic. He says something that challenges philosophy itself: 'if someone, having an eye on all the difficulties we have just brought up and others of the same sort, won't allow that there are forms for things and won't mark off a form for each one, he won't have anywhere to turn his thought, since he doesn't allow that for each thing there is a character that is always the same. In this way, he will destroy the power of *dialectic* entirely' (135b–c).

This is full of Platonic assumptions: the belief in a need for eternal and unchanging things, of things having an essential core (see page 19), of philosophy being only an essentially conceptual project, and that this is sufficient for giving us robust knowledge through the Forms (see page 13 and 24). Parmenides's surprising response seems to suggest that despite all the dialectical gymnastics that show the weaknesses of the theory, he still holds onto an *intuition* that agrees with Socrates about the Forms.

This shows the importance for Plato (and Plato's Parmenides) of *intuition* (or, feelings and opinions that we have about what is right or true) and that intuitions may have some priority over reason (see page 60 of Vol. 1 and 'Think: The Stimulus' and 'Summoners' on pages 10 and 11 of Vol. 2). Yet it is unclear whether Parmenides means *dialectic* in the technical or non-technical sense. And this ambiguity holds a key to how PhiE is derived from two senses of *dialectic* (see also page 47). The technical sense is the dizzying mathematical proof-like discourse that we see demonstrated in the latter part of the dialogue; the less technical sense is simply 'conversation'.

The *Parmenides* dialogue itself shows a distinction between two kinds of dialectic: *formal* and *informal* dialectic (or big 'D' dialectic and small 'd' dialectic - see page 47). The first of these we see properly and explicitly demonstrated in the exchanges between Parmenides and the young Aristotle (not the famous Aristotle!) at 187c–166c. The second can be seen in the earlier exchanges between Socrates, Zeno and Parmenides at 127d–137c. It is not difficult to see that the informal conversation is more natural, where respondents say a good deal more than Aristotle in the formal demonstration, and they respond with more than 'Yes', 'Necessarily', 'Why?' and so on; the formal demonstration is much more one-sided, even by Socratic standards! (See page xxxiii and 'Opening-up and Plato and Socrates' on page 49 of Vol. 2 for why Plato has this happen in his dialogues.)

It is also interesting that we do not see this kind of formal dialectic very much at all in Plato's dialogues; we see something much more akin to the informal kind, where the exchanges are more natural and, therefore, messier. Plato even has Parmenides explicitly refer to his formal demonstration of dialectic as, '. . . this strenuous game,' (137b) suggesting that it is forced and artificial.

So, why does Plato do this, if, as Parmenides says, the formal way is *the* way to solve problems, such as problems threatening the theory of Forms, no less? Could it merely be because dialogues written in the formal way would be less interesting to read? Or is there something more going on?

It is possibly because Plato is presenting this method of dialectic not as *the* model to be used but as something that *was* used, perhaps by Parmenides and his followers. In other words, it is being presented as *old fashioned*, and as something that is not quite up to the job of instantiating philosophical conversation. For instance, we already know that Socrates would not agree with the very first thing that is said, that, 'If it is one, the one would not be many, would it?' We know that he wouldn't agree because he has already drawn a distinction (129a–e) to explain how *one* can also be *many*.

He shows that they are – in more up-to-date terminology – *contraries* and not *contradictories*: a person can be many things: left arm, right arm, upper part and lower part . . . but may also be considered one thing, as a whole: a person. The young Aristotle, though, accepts what Parmenides says unquestioningly with a rhetorical question: 'No, how could it?' There is even a suggestion that Parmenides chooses Aristotle so that he may get away with things Socrates might not let him get away with when Parmenides says, 'Then who will answer my questions? The youngest, surely? For he would give the least trouble, and would be the most likely to say what he thinks. At the same time his answer would allow me a breathing space'. Contrast this with Socrates' comments about not letting himself get away with poor arguments when referring to 'Sophroniscus' son' in the *Hippias Major* (298c) on page 73 of Vol. 2.

Plato deliberately leaves the dialogue, at the conclusion of the demonstration, without returning to either of the two frames, also leaving it up to Socrates, the observer to the demonstration, and the reader – the observer of it all (see pages 2–3 of Vol. 1 and page 12 of Vol. 2) – to decide for themselves what they think of the quality and success of Parmenides' demonstration. This is where Plato's own dialectical pedagogy comes into play: triggering our own critical engagement with the issue by leaving the enquiries in some way unresolved for the reader to consider at a position of remove.

Plato famously had an inscription above the entrance to his academy, 'Let no one ignorant of geometry and mathematics enter'. This may suggest that Platonic dialectic could well have resembled the dry, geometrical method of Parmenides. However, his dialogues' starting point is modelled on Socrates. This meeting of Socratic and Platonic – and possibly Parmenidian – methods and aims means that their methods inform, and possibly limit, each other.

As with this historical meeting of methods, PhiE combines the technical sense of *dialectic* – or big 'D' Dialectic – with the more everyday use of the word *conversation*. PhiE is situated between high-end academic philosophical discourse and undisciplined chatter, or, to use Parmenides' words, '. . . idle talk' (135d). There is something of the freedom of a mere conversation, allowing – certainly at the earlier stages – the discussion to go in one direction, then another, for many different ideas to come in and possibly get in the way of others, for digressions to occur and so on. This is informal, small 'd' dialectic (see also page 87 of Vol. 2).

There is also a facilitator whose job it is to ensure that the dialectical considerations – including what follows from what, what meanings are being used, and what the consequences are of certain hypotheses – are attended to in a way appropriate to the group's level of ability and interest. PhiE is a convergence of these two, informal and formal dialectics: *conversational yet rigorous.*

Aristotle

Following the example of Socrates and Plato, Aristotle also turned his attention to philosophical method, developing on some of the ideas and practices of his predecessors and therefore progressing to the dialectical method of doing philosophy that underpins PhiE.

Aristotle holds on to all the main features of dialectic that McCabe identifies (see page 20): it remains logical, sequential, psychological, epistemological and normative, but he develops or contributes to how one conceives dialectic in the following ways.

For Plato, *dialectic* was a way for philosophers to reach robust knowledge directly, yet for Aristotle, who made important developments to empirical scientific investigation (see Leroi's *The Lagoon* 2014) 'dialectic probes where philosophy seeks understanding' (Metaphysics IV, 1004b, 25). Given what is said about PhiE's epistemological suspension on page 64, *understanding* is perhaps a more realistic aim for dialectic within PhiE than the harder-to-achieve Platonic aim of *robust knowledge*. Though, of course, dialectic, being based on truth-preserving discourse, may have a *role* to play in bringing one to knowledge in combination with other approaches, evidence and facts.

Aristotle's 'starting place' (or *archai*) for dialectic is *endoxa* or 'received opinions' (see also *doxa* on page 15). He also split this into two: the *common-sense opinions* of ordinary people and the *reputable opinions* of the wise; usually for Aristotle, 'the wise' were older philosophers such as Heraclitus, Socrates and Plato. It is very much in the spirit of PhiE, not only that Aristotle took the opinions of ordinary people seriously, *including* them, but that he also included 'the wise' – some practitioners of doing philosophy with children deliberately exclude the history of ideas altogether (see page 74 of Vol. 2).

Aristotle's overall aim was to put this aggregate of opinions through a systematic process of exploration and evaluation to both eliminate what was false or inconsistent and to preserve what was true and consistent among the opinions of both the ordinary people and the wise. Aristotle thought, therefore, that when engaging in a philosophical enquiry, the first thing to do was to survey the received opinions, or *endoxa*, systematically. This is still standard practice in universities today, particularly with reference to how general *intuitions* (what most would think and agree upon) and how classic *debates* and lines of argument within the literature are attended to.

In the classroom, it is relatively easy to have the pupils draw upon their own intuitions surrounding a question (see page 60 of Vol. 1 and pages 10, 65 and 89 of Vol. 2 for how to do this), but much harder to make them aware of the extant arguments and positions held by philosophers throughout history. Though it is not impossible to acquaint the pupils with the history of philosophy during a PhiE, there will, especially with the younger ones, be a limit to how much of this can be done before losing their engagement and therefore their attention in some way. This is one of the chief ways in which philosophy with children differs from philosophy with adults and professional philosophers: the extent to which they can or will engage with the history of ideas. (See pages 26 of Vol. 1 and 38 of Vol. 2 for how to include the history of ideas into a PhiE.)

Aristotle's next move is to see what problems (or, as he would call them, *aporai* – see pages 26 of Vol. 1 and 38 of Vol. 2) arise from or between the *endoxa*; to identify and outline any tensions, contradictions, inconsistencies and so on. The job of the philosopher, according to Aristotle, is to begin by *identifying* the 'knots' (the *aporai*) and then to attempt to *resolve* them, or to 'untie the knots' (Metaphysics B).

Aristotle and PhiE

Aristotle's outline of the dialectical process echoes the progress of Heraclitus' dialectical effect (see pages 15–17), describing a fairly natural psychological progress to a philosophical question. For this reason it resembles the progress taken by a class of children when they consider similar questions, with a little structural help from a facilitator. So, if the pupils are asked a question like 'Can you step into the same river twice?' the facilitator usually begins by gathering the pre-reflective intuitions about it, the *yeses* and the *noes*, the *maybes*, the *it depends*, the *boths* and so on. This corresponds with the Aristotelian *endoxa*, or at least the 'common sense of the ordinary people' understanding of it (see also Heraclitean *doxa* on page 15) and the Aristotelean notion of *phenomena*, or how things seem. One difference is that, in this case, one is working with the common-sense intuitions of the immediate group, rather than 'ordinary people' more generally.

Next, problems – or *aporai* – start to emerge from or between these starting intuitions, the clearest example of an *aporia* is an *apparent contradiction*; for example, *that it is and is not* possible to step into the same river twice (see pages 15–17). Some children will argue that it is possible and others that it's not, thereby instantiating a provisional and *apparent* paradox between their different and opposing views; it may turn out that it is not an *actual* paradox.

There are two ways that the pupils may begin to resolve any *aporai*: they may try to do so with whatever resources they have (the *implicit* approach) at their disposal, or the pupils may be introduced to skills and tools that they may be able to appeal to or apply (the *explicit* approach – see page 94 of Vol. 2). In either case, the sorts of moves the pupils might make include (among others) the *drawing of distinctions*, spotting and elucidating *ambiguities*, *interpreting* and *re-interpreting* a phrase or idea. And these are exactly the approaches Aristotle employs to resolve *aporai*.

It's important to know that Aristotle used the word *aporia* differently from Socrates. Whereas Socrates meant something like a psychological state of confusion or perplexity (see page 38 of Vol. 2), Aristotle used it to describe the problem or puzzle that faces the philosopher: the 'knot' that needs to be 'untied'; drawing on the myth about his famous pupil: 'Alexander the Great and the Gordian Knot'. Aristotle himself uses the analogy of a 'knot' that needs to be 'untied' for describing 'an aporia'.

Community of Enquiry

Philosophy for children (P4/wC) is often associated with a pedagogy called the 'community of inquiry' (CoI) or the 'community of philosophical inquiry' (CPI) and it has been claimed that PhiE '[does] not necessarily share commitment to the community of inquiry pedagogy or other Socratic methods of teaching *as an integral part* of using their texts' (Murris and Haynes 2016). So, what is a community of inquiry? Does PhiE follow a community of inquiry pedagogy? And how should 'e/inquiry' be spelt?

The ICPIC[17] website[18] says that CPI was originally developed by Lipman and Sharp and involves five stages:

1) The offering of the text: Students read or enact a philosophical story together.
2) The construction of the agenda: Students raise questions prompted by the text and organise them into a discussion agenda.
3) Solidifying the community: Students discuss their questions in a dialogue facilitated by an adult.
4) Using exercises and discussion plans: The facilitator introduces relevant activities to deepen and expand the students' inquiry.
5) Encouraging further responses: Students extend their inquiry through other activities, such as self-assessment of their philosophy practice, art projects and action projects.

PhiE certainly fits with the broader notion of a community of inquiry in that PhiE is a 'collection of individuals who jointly embark on an empirical and/or conceptual process of inquiry into problematic areas of consideration or situations' (Wikipedia: 'Community of Inquiry' – see Bibliography). But PhiE does not fit so comfortably with 1 (above), the stimulus is not always a text, nor is it necessarily read or enacted; nor does it fit with 2, not because PhiE participants do not construct the agenda, but that they do not do so according to the standard P4/wC method (see 'Introduction to PhiE' footnote 2 on page xxxiv); and 5, because PhiE is a dialectical method of doing philosophy, it does not set itself up as a platform for political activism; some participants may, of course, be motivated to action following an enquiry *but it is not a part of the PhiE method to include this*, and if it is a part of a CoI to include this, then PhiE diverges from a CoI in this way.

In order to explain the PhiE notion of a community of philosophical enquiry (note spelling change), rather than turning to the usual suspects: Peirce, Dewey and Lipman, I have been showing how PhiE's understanding of this concept is built from ancient Greek ideas. Apart from the differences noted above, the reason for doing this is that the pragmatist understanding of a CoI has led to some unhelpful tendencies, albeit unintended consequences.

The strong association that CoI has with democracy sometimes leads teachers and participants of P4/wC to some mistaken views: either that there is no knowledge in a CoI, only opinions, or that knowledge is *decided upon* by the group through a group consensus. (See McCall on page 63.)

Teachers and facilitators of P4/wC often tell classes that 'philosophy has no right and wrong answers' (see also pages 11–12 of Vol. 1 and pages 24 and 27 of Vol. 2) or that 'your opinions cannot be wrong', or 'there are lots of good answers', and other similar phrases. Again, this is done for perfectly understandable reasons, such as that they may want to give the pupils the confidence to speak in front of their peers, but it can lead to the view that communities of inquiry are nothing more than collections of individual subjective beliefs and that knowledge is irreducibly *multiplist* (subjective, relative and plural – see page 25 of Vol. 2).

The accompanying worry is that, far from being the antidote to 'post-truth' anxieties, P4/wC is, inadvertently, exacerbating them. PhiE works hard to counter this tacit assumption (see pages 27 and 94 of Vol. 2), so, though I will hang on to the notion of a 'community of inquiry', I, to some extent, attempt to extricate it from the long association it has with the American pragmatists. So that I may separate what I am talking about from the usual CoI, I will spell enquiry with an 'e' (CoE). (For more on the epistemology underlying PhiE see page 63.)

Firstly, I would argue that the dialogues of Plato often instantiate and model communities of enquiry, and, at their best, show us an ideal model of how a community of enquiry may best proceed (usefully, we also see examples of how *not* to proceed or behave in a community of enquiry[19]). This book draws much of its good practice from that of Socrates and others in Platonic dialogues and earlier examples, and the best practice is not to be found in any one place, in any one dialogue or uniformly throughout the dialogues (see page 20) but is drawn from disparate places from many different dialogues. This is especially the case given that the dialogues have so many aims: philosophical, pedagogical, literary, political and historical – at least! (See pages xx and xxxiii.)

Let's begin with 'enquiry'. A contemporary of Socrates, Herodotus used the word *historie* to describe what he was doing when he wrote his account – the *Histories* – of the Persian Wars (between Greece and Persia), and the word *historie* here means 'inquiry' rather than what we take it to mean today. Also, Herodotus' structural approach to inquiry in some way fits with PhiE's informal dialectical approach (see pages 22–24), with its digressions and pauses, while still having its eye on a main thread. The *Histories* has been described as resembling a washing line (Higgins 2008) in that there is a main thread with 'fairly substantial, self-contained items hanging off it' (ibid.).

For the idea of *community*, I will turn to the notion of the ancient Greek *polis*. A *polis* is usually thought of as a 'city state', but this raises philosophical questions as to what comprises a city state. Higgins (2008) identifies a common, misleading translation of a well-known quote by Aristotle: 'Man is by nature a political animal' (*Politics*). But, as she points out, the way we might understand this in modern English is not how it was meant by Aristotle. It does not mean that people naturally involve themselves in matters of the state, but that 'man by nature is an animal *fitted to living in a polis*' (ibid.). And, by *polis*, is meant something like a 'community', and a Greek *polis* was a self-governing (autonomous) community (see page 34).

To complete the idea, the *polis* (certainly the Athenian *polis*) is not to be thought of as merely what lies within the city walls, but, as the general Nicias was reported to have said by Thucydides in his book *The History of the Peloponnesian War*, 'It is men who make the city [*polis*] and not walls or ships with no men inside them'.

A community of enquiry then, is – as Higgins describes ancient Greece itself in the introduction to her book *It's All Greek to Me* – '. . . not simply . . . a specific place or time, but a realm where the imagination ... and the intellect can roam free,' where the aim is to 'know thyself' (as the inscription at the Oracle of Delphi enjoined us to do) as well as the world and each other, despite – and perhaps *because of* – the holes and gaps in our knowledge and understanding (see pages 9–11). And, as Higgins says about Plato's dialogues, the community of enquiry's 'very form encapsulates disagreement, debate and provisional answers rather than unshakeable dogma,' (see 'Two-eyed thinking' on pages 6–7). 'Incompleteness,' says Higgins, '. . . is at its heart', or, coming back to philosophy itself, 'Philosophy is defined by what it lacks'.

We can, perhaps, capture what a community of enquiry is, then, through a Platonic notion of justice (with qualifications), especially as Plato drew this from a comparison between the soul and the Greek city state (*polis*), similarly to how I have drawn a notion of *community* from the *polis*. A community of enquiry, as with 'justice' in the *Republic*, 'consists in each part performing its appropriate task (441d–e). Its essence is unity: . . . mak[ing] one "[become] entirely one from many" (443e)' (Pappas 2003).

A community of enquiry is not *prescriptive* about this, but *descriptive* (see page 52): it allows for a particular kind of intellectual personality to step forward when the situation lends itself to a particular way of thinking. In any group there will be cynics, sceptics, those that tend towards logical thinking, critical thinking, creative thinking, lateral thinking, there may be those that tend towards the seeking of counterexamples, those that like to draw distinctions, make analogies or take a synoptic view (see pages 21 and 68 of Vol. 1 and page 30 of Vol. 2) and so on and so forth.

A PhiE provides opportunities for all these different kinds of thinkers to play a role in approaching the question or problem (see 'Excellence' on page 41), as and when they are self-motivated to do so (see 'Love of learning' on page 9), where self-motivation becomes responsive to the demands of the enquiry at any one time. Introducing a metacognitive aspect to a PhiE (see page 94 of Vol. 2) can also help the group to deliberate about which of these kinds of thinking or related strategies may be the most appropriate at any given time.

For instance, the Imaginary Disagreer (see page 74 of Vol. 2) is a powerful way to actively invoke the different thinking personalities within a community of enquiry. For instance, one of the variations of this strategy is to invoke an absent member , 'What would X say about this if s/he were here?' (see page 76 of Vol. 2). This is an example of how a particular way of thinking can be called upon during an enquiry but it also helps to ensure that the virtues of a particular individual can be transferred and assimilated into the group as a whole so that 'having come from many things, [the community[20]] becomes . . . one' (*Republic* 443d–e).

NOTES

1. See also 'What Is "Philosophy"? Understandings of Philosophy Circulating in the Literature on the Teaching and Learning of Philosophy in Schools', by Lynne Bowyer et al. (2020).

2. Take a look at the many answers philosophers give to this here: https://www.brainpickings.org/2012/04/09/what-is-philosophy/.

3. My own short definition of philosophy is inspired by Sellars': 'philosophy is everything, within reason'.

4. https://aeon.co/essays/without-conversation-philosophy-is-just-dogma.

5. Here is a Tedx talk I gave explaining the four 'R's at Goodenough College in 2014: https://www.youtube.com/watch?v=dQzK4XCXV7c.

6. Thanks to Ilse Daems for the phrase 'thinking the unthinkable', the title of the 2019 SOPHIA network meeting in Galway, Ireland.

8. Also of different cultures (see Introduction pages xxviii–xxix).

8. This is not available outside of the UK.

9. See also the graphic novel *Unflattening* (2015) by Nick Sousanis, which argues for the necessity of simultaneously inhabiting more than one position. Thomas Wartenberg discusses this in his forthcoming book *Philosophy Illustrated*.

10. For a longer list go here: https://www.academia.edu/33553846/Intellectual_virtues_of_doing_philosophy.

11. A preface or preamble to a book or long speech.

12. From McCabe (1982, 2015) *Parmenides' Dilemma* (footnote 7).

13. Fragment translations derived from M.M. McCabe (1988, 2015), Jonathan Barnes (1987) and Pamela Mensh (Miller 2018).

14. Chapter 1, 'Platonic Conversations' in *Platonic Conversations* by Mary Margaret McCabe (2015).

15. Candidate *elenctic* dialogues include, in addition to the *Euthyphro*, the *Laches*, the *Lysis* and the *Charmides*.

16. Many children (and some adults!) also have a tendency to answer a 'What is X?' question with examples and not general definitions.

17. The International Council of Philosophical Inquiry with Children.

18. https://my.icpic.org/about.html

19. Examples: Thrasymachus in *Republic* and Euthydemus and Dionysodorus in *Euthydemus*.

20. Plato says 'he', meaning 'the just person'. I have co-opted the phrase to mean 'the community of enquiry'.

Part Two

Core Values of PhiE

ANCIENT CORE VALUES OF PHIE

Edith Hall, in her book *The Ancient Greeks: Ten Ways They Shaped the Modern World* (2015), identifies ten core values at the heart of ancient Greek culture. I find these helpful, not only for understanding the ancient Greeks but also for showing how important aspects of doing philosophy can be found in a Greek understanding of life more generally. This comes of the Greek emphasis on philosophy as *ethos*, or 'way of life', something that is pursued as an *activity,* not just learnt about at school or university (see also Pierre Hadot's book *What Is Ancient Philosophy?* on philosophy as *ethos*).

The Greeks spoke of *techne* (skills) and *hexis* (disposition), and philosophy; 'the Greek way', is not intended merely to be a skill, it is dispositional and therefore *a way of being*: informing how we see and how we think, but also informing how we see and think *about* how we see and think.

To help us outline what this way of being is, here are Hall's ten features of the ancient Greeks:

- *Seafaring*
- *Suspicion of authority*
- *Individual freedom*
- *Inquiring minds*
- *Openness*
- *Humour*
- *Competition*
- *Excellence*
- *Articulacy*
- *Pleasure*

Hall's list can be 'translated' into one more appropriate for PhiE's core values. Here they are followed by some explanatory notes:

- **Exploration** (Hall's *Seafaring*)
- **Dissent** (*Suspicion of authority*)
- **Autonomy** (*Individual freedom*)
- **Enquiry** (*Inquiring minds*)
- **An open, questioning mindset** (*Openness*)
- **Friendship** (*Humour, pleasure*)
- **Excellence** (*Competition, excellence*)
- **Oracy** (*Articulacy*)

Let's look at each of these in more detail and see how they fit with PhiE.

Exploration and Discovery (Seafaring)

Given the ancient Greek love of analogy (see page 36 below), it is appropriate to think of the philosophical community in a PhiE as being like the crew of a ship. The *sea* may stand for *the world/reality*; the *crew* for the *class or participants* who bring their various insights, talents and idiosyncrasies to bear on the problem; and *the captain* stands for *the facilitator* who has some knowledge of philosophy and how philosophical method can be implemented. Also, when at sea, there is no clear path to follow, neither for the captain nor the crew, the direction has to be determined or discovered by those on board.

Eschewing any further seafaring similes (which may seem a little stretched at this point), this can in general translate to the notion of *exploration*, and perhaps also *discovery*. My colleague Pieter Mostert, during a presentation for TPF, divided philosophy into two parts: the *exploratory* and the *justificatory*. I re-present the distinction here as I find it useful for practitioners new to facilitating philosophy. PhiE begins with the *exploratory aspect*. Here we say what we think, try things out, possibly contradict ourselves and change our minds. It can be a messy process, inconclusive and sometimes lacking in cogency.

If you are signed up to the dialectical model of doing philosophy presented in this book, you may be forgiven for thinking that philosophy is *all and only* about arguments, reasoning, critical thinking, cogency and so on, and of course, these are important, but we must not forget that there is much more to philosophy than this. (See pages 1–6 and page 28.)

Philosophy problems begin in our pre-reflective intuitions or 'gut instincts' (see page 60), and, certainly when doing philosophy in groups, this is almost necessarily exploratory and pre-reasoned. It is only in our attempts to solve, make sense of or explain those problems that we must move towards *ordering* our thinking.

The second aspect is the *justificatory aspect*. This is where we try to make a case, to say what we think is true (or false), possible (or impossible), plausible (or implausible), right (or wrong), coherent (or incoherent), and to do so we must argue for *why* (in the justificatory sense, see page 21 of Vol. 2) we think something true, possible, plausible, right, coherent and so on. (See page 24 of Vol. 2 for more nuances about justificatory thinking.)

Returning – if I may – to the seafaring comparisons, today, we might say, 'Everyone should learn to read and write'; the Greeks said, 'Everyone should learn to read and swim' (Hall 2015). We take swimming for granted, as most westerners learn to swim while young, but back then it was unusual for anyone to learn to swim and the Greeks were quite unique in being able to not only swim (and dive) from an early age but in prizing it so highly. It is easy to feel like one is sinking while attempting to do something like philosophy or that one is without air (see page 38 of Vol. 2), and so the skills are needed to be able to at least keep one's head above the water, but perhaps also to be able to do without air for longer, and to move forward with purpose and direction (see page 35 of Vol. 2). One needs to learn to swim philosophically.

Dissent (Suspicion of Authority)

A great deal has been made about the collaborative qualities of doing philosophy in schools, but what is sometimes overlooked (perhaps, because of its non-conductivity to the promotion of philosophy in a state-approved programme of education) is philosophy's *subversiveness*. However, because of PhiE's explicit placement within the Socratic tradition, and given that Socrates was put on trial, found guilty and executed for 'corrupting the minds of the young and preaching false gods' (see book title and 'Preface' on pages xv–xvii), the subversive aspect cannot – and *should* not – be overlooked.

In the UK, P4/wC has, to some extent, been appropriated by a government-sanctioned movement to promote 'British values'[1] as part of the Prevent agenda[2] (2011). And whatever you think about the chosen list of British values (democracy, rule of law, individual liberty and mutual respect and tolerance of those with different faiths), surely a missing – *central* – value associated with British and American history and history of ideas is 'dissent'. From the UK perspective, just think of Henry the VIII's break away from Rome, or the church of 'dissenters', the challenge to the throne that resulted in the English Civil War and the removal of the monarch, the philosophy of Hume and Russell, the plays (and characters) of Shakespeare and the works of Swift, the Brontës, George Eliot, Wells and Orwell, among many others. It won't be difficult to come up with a similar list from American history.

This does not mean that PhiE sees itself in an antithetical or antagonistic relationship with the education system in which it finds itself, just that it can be an important way for any education system to ensure that it is giving expression to that essential value of any democratic education system, namely: *dissent*. And perhaps because of PhiE's minimal commitment to democracy (see page 62), it is better placed than those more extensively committed to democratic ideology to resist current trends such as the Prevent agenda and thereby fulfil the dissenting aspect of democracy.

A PhiE facilitator does not try to bring a group to consensus as a point of principle (as Nelsonian Socratic Dialogue does), or to draw all members of the community towards an agreed group-answer (for instance, when a teacher says, 'So, last week we agreed that working together is better than doing things alone'), but actively seeks out the dissenting views, allowing the awkward questions to be asked, welcoming controversy and including the 'annoying kid at the back of the class'.[3] The four Cs of P4/wC are *critical, creative, collaborative* and *caring* thinking. PhiE certainly endorses the first three of these (see page 28 in Vol. 2 for a discussion of the fourth, *caring thinking*), but brings the critical and collaborative together as dialectical dance partners, describing PhiE as 'critically collaborative' and 'collaboratively critical'.

What is meant by this is that a PhiE community collaborates in its enquiries, and a central feature of collaborating is to question, challenge and critique, so that collaborating and critiquing are, yin-yang-like, mutually integrative: when you collaborate, you should critique, and when you critique, you should do so as part of a collaborative effort. Elsewhere, I have put it in concise but pompous Hegelian language: *philosophy is the synthesis of collaboration and opposition* par excellence.[4]

Autonomy (Individual Freedom)

So, following the 'Dissent' entry, short of being a kind of nihilistic 'punk' movement in education, philosophy should be a space as independent from thought-control and propaganda as possible; a place where the pupils' autonomy can be flexed and freedom of thought and expression given free rein (or as much as possible) in an environment that is healthily sceptical but not cynical. A PhiE is a place where the usual figures of intellectual authority – teachers and adults – suspend their authority in certain key respects while inviting the pupils to turn to themselves as a group (see pages 67–76) and their own thinking abilities as resources for tackling questions, problems and puzzles.[5] Instead, the teachers *as facilitators* inhabit a guiding, structural role, helping realise a very Greek idea: *freedom within discipline*.

Socrates (and those that followed him) was around during a period of history known as *The Axiel Age*, in which he is joined by other luminaries such as Confucius and Loa Tzu in China, Buddha and the Advaita Vedanta movement in India. This age seemed to usher in a new kind of human consciousness. It is difficult to pinpoint exactly what it was that brought this about, but it certainly seems to have corresponded with the emergence of the 'individual' within society. The Greeks epitomised this shift in their art, theatre and politics and, of course, their philosophy. Socrates' injunction to examine oneself inwardly, 'the unconsidered life is not a human life'[6] (Plato's *Apology*), and his own effortful act of self-creation and refinement (see page xxxii) mark this shift very explicitly.

But this individualism is not the narcissistic, selfish individualism of today. Coming, as it did, out of an earlier consciousness characterised by a collective identity, it clung to collective notions of identity. The new political shift towards what we know as 'democracy' embodied the meeting of these two kinds of consciousness: this new Greek ideal, *demokratia*, was the synthesis of the individual and the collective, the individual understood as both a singular entity but also as part of a group entity where its members are interdependent upon one another. As Charlotte Higgins says, 'The buzz words of the time [in ancient Greece during the emergence of democracy] were *isegoria* – freedom of speech; and *isonomia* – equality before the law' (2008).

This notion of the individual gave rise to a new idea: *individual freedom*, that Hall identifies as one of 'the ten', and this in turn gave rise to *individual agency* and therefore to *individual responsibility* which would eventually give us *ethics* and *morality*, both of which are central to many later religions, and the concern of philosophy for millennia to this day.[7] PhiE, therefore, does not see the community engaged in enquiry as merely a collection of individuals, but as a conglomeration of individuals within a group, the freedom of each being understood in relation to the other(s) (see 'Community of Enquiry' on pages 26–30).

So, in a PhiE one is free to speak, but one may be held to account (see Oracy on page 44 below); one may be free to defend a position, but a position may only be defended if it can be shown to be *defensible*. It is the community's duty to test a position's defensibility or search for a defence not hitherto thought of. It is freedom, but it is a regulated freedom, limited by an idealised reasonableness realised by the group and its facilitator. (See pages 58 and 71.)

Inquiry/Enquiry[8] (Inquiring Minds)

As far as we know, the Greeks were the first – certainly in Europe – to use purely rational means to inquire about the world, beginning a move away from the traditional reliance on mythological and religious explanations for natural phenomena (although, of course, they had these kinds of explanations as well – see page 8). And, insofar as PhiE understands philosophy as *at least* (but not only) a rational project, it remains a descendent of this innovation. Hall (2015) identifies four key Greek intellectual characteristics associated with inquiry that we also find in PhiE.

Firstly, she says that it was the Greeks' development of language, or, their 'flexible tongue . . . that gave them a wider range than most modern languages of ways to express causality, consequence, and sophisticated grades of overlap between them' (see Oracy on page 44 below). PhiE begins, as does P4/wC more broadly, with the assumption that philosophy can be done with and through ordinary language (see page xxx), as the Greeks believed, but that one must learn to use, manipulate and shape the words and language at one's disposal to be able to give expression to difficult and complex ideas. This is done individually but also between members of a PhiE community.

Perhaps at odds with Plato, but with Socrates, PhiE thinks that there is no need for familiarity with a lexicon of technical language to be able to begin doing philosophy. That is not to say that there is *no* place for more technical philosophy, just that it is not necessary to be able to *do* philosophy. This is very important for being able to do philosophy with children and non-philosopher adults. That said, PhiE is not averse to introducing some history, technical terminology and some philosophical methods to the group (see page 87 of Vol. 2 for more on this), and it sometimes does so, albeit in a measured way 'by such reasons as [the participants'] age and understanding are capable of' (Locke 1996 – see also page 51).

Secondly, Hall identifies a Greek *love of analogy* ('X is like Y'); something that is very common in the way children (above a certain age) think and express themselves. Looking at the transcripts I've made of philosophy sessions with 10- and 11-year-olds,[9] a very common response structure, for example, to a Task Question such as 'Does Og [the cave-person] own the land that he/she has fenced off?' is: 'I think Og does/does not own the land because it's like when . . . [analogy is made as a reason]' For many children, analogy is a primary reason-giving mode (see pages xvii–xviii of Vol. 1 for different reason-giving modes).

Hall's third characteristic of inquiry is, appropriately, the opposite of this: their *love of polarity* ('X is the opposite of Y'). This third, when taken alongside Hall's fourth, *the unity of opposites* (see pages 4–5), is itself an expression of the fourth characteristic. Despite their association with rationality, the Greeks were great lovers of *paradox*, one of them being their proclivity towards both *rationality*: order, form, proportion (the Apollonian – see page 8) and *irrationality*: chaos, the emotions and instincts (Dionysian[10]). It is therefore no surprise that Plato has been given both rationalist and mystical readings, humanist and religious.

One can also see how PhiE instantiates these elements in that PhiE begins with the paradox-inducing question, like Heraclitus (see page 15), where an attempt to make sense of the paradox is made, usually through nuanced distinction-drawing or re-interpretation. (See pages 15–16 and 26 for more on this.)

An Open, Questioning Mindset (Openness)

Hall recognises that the value of openness in Greek society (particularly Athenian society) is not straightforward. Yes, they were open, as Hall says, 'to innovation, to adopting ideas from outside, and to self-expression', they welcomed immigrants and allowed 'honest examination of emotions and human behaviour in the theatre and in philosophy'. But this value of openness is also identifiable in Athenian culture by its limitations and the debates surrounding its delimitation: they were often discussing how far the freedoms and amenities of the city should be made available to outsiders, and, of course, Socrates was put to death for questioning people too much.

Likewise, philosophy is also something which encourages openness to new ideas and criticism, but it also insists on critical thinking criteria to delimit those ideas, recognising that it is not enough merely to say what we think, we must do so cogently and show how what we are saying is true or for what reasons it should be taken seriously. In other words, philosophy is open, but not so open that it is rendered empty, worthless or absurd. (See also pages 11, 28, 65, 73.) The ideal philosopher says, 'I would like to *hear* what you have to say and I will do my best to *understand* what you have to say, but I will respond in a way that will *test* what you've said to see how *robust* it is'.

So, openness is understood in PhiE not only by the need or celebration of it, but by its reasonable – and contestable – limits. This book contains a great deal about what I have called an Open Questioning Mindset (OQM – see page 71), but here I mean something informal, less technical, distinguished from OQM by the placement of a comma, a hyphen and the removal of capital letters: *an open, questioning mind-set.*

Friendship (Humour, Pleasure)

One of the ten principles conferred to us by the ancient Greeks (see page 31), according to Hall, is their *love of pleasure*. The idea of the *symposium*, or 'drinking party' (the best example of which comes to us through Plato in his dialogue *Symposium*[11]) blends the Greek love of pleasure with their love of inquiry. Short of bringing alcohol into the classroom (!), a similar thing is done – and *must* be done – when doing philosophy with the young in PhiE. Providing the intellectual conditions (see pages 56–58) for the necessary intellectual desire to occur (e.g., questions that produce a dialectical effect) is essential, but there's more that's needed.

The members of the group need to feel part of a community, to enjoy what they are doing together, to trust one another, to derive mutual pleasure from what they are doing and to have fun (see comments about enjoyment and engagement on page 55).

In previous publications (Worley 2011, 2019b), I have already drawn on the figure of Ariadne as an emblematic figure for facilitating philosophy (also see page 67), having Theseus stand in for the 'participants' of a philosophical enquiry, the labyrinth for 'philosophy' and Ariadne for the 'facilitator'. And as well as being the goddess of the Labyrinth, she was, through her association with Dionysus, also the goddess of the Dance. This is appropriate, because there is a sense in which doing philosophy together is a 'dance through the labyrinth of thought'; dancing, after all, should have a dialectical (question-and-answer) – but also pleasurable – motion to it.

AN EPICUREAN GARDEN IN SCHOOL

It is common for schools to feature gardens as something to support learning or personal growth. There are 'peace gardens', 'growing gardens', 'play gardens', 'friendship gardens' and so on. Quite apart from his refreshingly un-ageist take on philosophy, 'Let no one put off studying philosophy when he is young, nor, when old, grow weary of its study,'[1] the Hellenistic philosopher, Epicurus, offers a recommendation for both a literal and figurative 'garden' as 'a place to do philosophy' with 'friends'.

First, *literally*: somewhere between 341 and 270 BCE, he established what today we would describe as a 'commune': a place where he lived with friends in self-sufficiency and contemplation known as 'The Garden'. It was in this 'Epicurean garden' that they conversed with one another, studied together, and ate simple food they had grown or made themselves. What PhiE gets from this is the idea of *ideal conditions* for doing philosophy communally .

Second, *metaphorically*: the '*Epicurean Garden*' stands for these ideal conditions under which a community of people may engage in philosophical conversations in a particular kind of place and in a particular kind of relationship to one another; as 'friends'. And by 'friends' I do not mean 'best buddies', but a relationship of mutual, respectful *consideration* (see page 28 in Vol. 2 for more on this concept) of one another's ideas, of being both supportive and critical in search of 'the most reasonable answer(s)' (Reznitskaya and Wilkinson 2017) to questions and problems under consideration by the group. But 'friends' also means a relationship that engenders or allows for (appropriate) laughter, humour, fun and pleasure (see above). Appropriately, the etymology of the word *philosophy* shows that the word for 'friendship' (*philia*) lies latent within it.

On pages 56–60 of Vol. 1 and pages xxiii–xxvi of Vol. 2, I look more closely at what these conditions might be and how we can best achieve them in the school environment, what we can control and what we cannot.

[1]Letter to Menoeceus (O'Connor 1993).

Friendship: Xenia and Knowing Thyself

Of the many words for *love* that the ancient Greeks had (compared to English's one!), such as *eros* (sexual love), *philia* (friendship-love or love of pursuits), *agape* (loving kindness towards all humankind), *storge* (love of one's family), *philautia* (love of oneself, either positively – 'necessary self-care' or negatively – 'narcissism'), among the most overlooked is *xenia*.[12] Deriving from the ancient Greek word for 'stranger', and more familiar to many in its negative form *xenophobia* ('fear or hatred of the stranger'), this meant 'care of the stranger' or 'guest-friendship' and contained the ancient Greek concept of *hospitality*.

According to this principle and tradition, which the Greeks probably inherited from the Egyptians, strangers would be welcomed into one's home and offered food and drink. Functionally, this was an important part of how news was carried, particularly concerning what was happening in foreign lands. So, as one may imagine, *conversation* would play an important role in this exchange.

There are several senses in which PhiE expresses *xenia*. The backgrounds to PhiE – for example, School – are often, *in a sense,* a coming together of 'strangers': most of the children in a class are not friends before they are brought together, and many will never become *close* friends, thus requiring all kinds of social and interpersonal negotiations between the members of the class. Also, a school can be a place where different cultures and religions meet; indeed, it may be one of the only places some children mix with children of different backgrounds. And in addition, this 'coming together' is done within an expectation of mutual respect, listening and cultural exchange,[13] or, in another word: *xenia*.

There is also a more philosophical sense in which the members of a PhiE express *xenia* in that their 'philosophical selves' are unknown – and therefore strangers – to one another. 'The moral self' (or *what one thinks is the right thing to do and what principles govern this*), and 'the epistemological self' (or *how one thinks we come to know things and what principles govern that*) are either unknown to one another or at least not sufficiently understood.

To begin approaching the knowability of 'the other', and thereby beginning a motion towards dissolving the boundary between the self and the other, PhiE engages the participants in a project of empathy and (critical) understanding. This is done through the sharing of ideas and proper engagement with those ideas while aiming at better understanding of oneself, each other and the world around us, something that goes both inwards and outwards (Hadot's philosophical practice of 'concentration' and 'expansion of the self' – 2002). The tools for doing so are *words* and *dialectical reasoning* or, put another way: *language* and *systematic thought* (see Parmenides' conditions for dialectic on pages 12–13).

Central to optimising this aim, is good *listening* (see page 27 of Vol. 2) and proper *consideration* (see page 28 of Vol. 2). To provide the conditions for these, PhiE must begin with a certain beginning attitude towards the 'strangers' with whom the participants find themselves asked to think both deeply and personally, and with whom they are asked to share their world view, something probably viewed only opaquely by themselves, let alone others.

This being the final meaning of *xenia*: that we are, to some extent, *strangers to ourselves*. Given that many responses to *why* questions are reporting tentative beliefs rather than robust justifications of invested beliefs (see page 24 of Vol. 2), what participants undergo during a PhiE, or a course of PhiE sessions, is a process of *discovery*. Discovering what they think about things, and what their justifications for those things in fact are, sometimes finding themselves at odds with what they think and why they think it, and therefore finding themselves re-thinking their own position in light of what others (or they) have said (see 'Re-Evaluation' on page 4).

Perhaps they will discover what their (and their peers') own epistemology – or theory of knowledge – is, and perhaps they will even revise this too, realising that one's epistemology is itself dynamic (see pages 25–26 of Vol. 2). PhiE precipitates a discovery of one's 'philosophical self'. The spirit of *xenia* in PhiE demands that we learn to accommodate not only 'the strangers' that are the other members of the group, but also – and of at least equal importance – the stranger that is *one's self*.

There is a final twist to this story. As Julian Baggini puts it in his book, *How the World Thinks*, 'we cannot understand ourselves if we do not understand others'. And what it means is that the 'guest-friendship' of PhiE is not a mere politeness, it is a necessary step towards self-knowledge. Or, as the Southern African *Ubuntu* philosophy would have it: 'I am because we are'.[14] See page 34 for how, in philosophy, collaboration necessarily implies criticism, bearing a similar relationship to that of the self and the other.

Excellence (Hall's Excellence, Competition)

The Greeks loved competition and the pursuit of excellence: they were fascinated by, for instance, the most *beautiful* (Helen of Troy), the most *resourceful* (Odysseus), the *wisest* (Socrates, according to the Oracle at Delphi),[15] the *strongest* (Heracles) and the *fastest* (Achilles). For many, this is the most problematic of the Greek values for today as the word *excellence* is associated with the word *elite*. However, it is important not to conflate these concepts. A related word, *competition* is another that sits uncomfortably with modern educational values, as *winners* imply *losers*, and in today's 'everyone's-a-winner' culture, there's no time for losers.

PhiE welcomes both excellence and competition, but not without qualification. PhiE seeks the best – meaning 'the most reasonable' (Reznitskaya & Wilkinson 2017) – answers and for this the group needs to excel. The group will excel, it will be *the* best it can be, if its members excel, if they perform at *their* best (see the Platonic aspect of a community of enquiry on page 29). In my experience of many years doing philosophy in schools, children of all ability levels can contribute important yet different insights and ideas that further the enquiry in significant and various ways, whether that is a reasoning insight, a creative one, a social one, or in some other way.

So, excellence does not necessarily imply exclusion (as *elite* does) nor does it appeal only to the higher ability children (as *elite* does), PhiE seeks an excellence within each individual child or participant (according to a relative scale internal to each individual) *in addition to* the excellence of the highest performers (according to a more external scale).

PhiE does not neglect the *evaluative* and *eliminative* aspects (see page 25 of Vol. 2) of doing dialectical philosophy. For instance, if a child says, in response to the question, 'What is real?' something like, 'For something to be real it has to have a heartbeat', although it is accepted by PhiE that the child *has the right* to say this and the child's opinion is valued (that is: *properly considered* – see page 28 of Vol. 2), it does not mean that the child's opinion is protected from error or criticism; and the child's statement in this case needs to be subjected to criticism.

So, when another child responds by saying, 'I disagree because a table is real but it doesn't have a heartbeat', he or she has successfully provided a counterexample to the statement, therefore revealing its error. Dialectically speaking, the error should be addressed, either by *revising* the statement or by *rejecting* it and starting again.

If PhiE is evaluative/eliminative (see page 25 of Vol. 2), then it follows that answers must in some way *compete*. That is not to say that PhiE is reduced to a competitive debate or game, there are after all, appropriate and inappropriate ways to foster competition, but PhiE is not as squeamish about competition as some educational initiatives today. Due to the prominence of proper reasoning in PhiE, it implies an aspect of 'healthy competition', so, if the culture is right (see page 59), if the participants trust the format, the facilitator and the quality of the criteria (i.e., reasoning, openness and defeasibility), then there is no reason to suppose that any healthy competition present in a search for a best answer will be – in a way harmful to the enquiry – negatively felt.

EXCELLENCE AND COMPETITION:
THE PARADOX OF SOCRATES

One of the most difficult squares-to-be-circled when thinking about Socrates as a source for doing philosophy with children, or as an emblematic figure, is whether he was the truth-seeker he claimed to be, in contrast to the Sophists, or whether he was a Sophist himself, with his eyes on the prize of 'winning the argument'?

The Sophists were a group of philosophers extant at the time of Socrates who would take money to teach people the art of rhetoric so that they could speak in front of large numbers of people and so win them over with political speeches. Socrates objected to this, saying it was inimical to the higher value of truth-seeking. (See in particular Plato's *Gorgias*, *Protagoras*, *Sophist* and *Euthydemus* dialogues, each of which includes an important Sophist as a character.)

Distinguishing Socrates from the Sophists is not as easy as one might think, despite how Socrates is consistently pitted against them, and in the *Sophist* dialogue the difference between them is said to be as little as the difference between dogs and wolves (231a). Perhaps the difference between them lies in the intention one has (to understand or to win – see page 53) and the attitude one has towards one's interlocutor or opponent, whether one treats their ideas fairly and attempts to understand and uncover their intended meaning rather than, legalistically, holding them to the surface meaning of their utterances (see page 74).

P4/wC is often associated with 'the four Cs': *creative, critical, collaborative*, and *caring thinking*, and it is easy to see how Socrates exemplifies the first two, but less easy to see how he exemplifies the last two. It is often said that Socrates preferred the *dialectic* (collaborative) mode of conversation over the *eristic*[1] (combative) mode of the Sophists, but does his practice bear this out? Many would describe Socrates as a model philosophical investigator, but many also see him as a 'bully' and competitive 'pugilist' in conversation. This is the paradox of Socrates, but is it possible to resolve this? Yes, and it can be done, once again, by appeal to the *unity of opposites* (see pages 4–5). First of all, Socrates's biography:

D'angour (2019) identifies how Socrates would have been brought up, like every other well-to-do Athenian boy, with the ambition to be a hero, and so his youth would have been spent seeking glory in athletic games, on the battlefield, in poetry, drama and even philosophy, which was primarily proto-science at that time. As well as being educated in poetry and music, he would also have been educated in gymnastics, athletics and wrestling (Plato, for instance, was a good wrestler). These would have been very common ambitions in young Greek men. Socrates, having gained some glory on the battlefield as a young man, at some point in his later life, changed and renounced the usual trappings of being a successful Greek man and instead turned to a life of philosophical contemplation and investigation in search of philosophical knowledge.

These humbler characteristics that we associate with Socrates were also present in stories told by his contemporary, Herodotus, for example, contrasting the high-life with the more self-effacing, reflective life – see, for example, the story of Solon and King Croesus of Lydia, *Histories* Book 1: 29–33. So, following a suggestion by D'Angour, it's not that there was one ambitious man, and then there was another more intellectually orientated man; these 'two' men collided, the one informing the other.

Socrates *the elder*, though in service to knowledge-seeking, would still bear the characteristics of Socrates *the younger*, the wannabe hero. And we see this in the dialogues themselves. We see a man bent on seeking truth, but also willing to fight for it; he has become the unity of these two supposed opposites. So, at his best, Socrates *is* a collaborative thinker, but Plato is not afraid to let us see a less collaborative side; and he is also a robust thinker, who will not let a bad idea survive or a good idea go where the reasons support this. He did become something of a hero, albeit in a very different way to the Homeric hero he would have wanted to be as a younger man, and he is now probably the most well-known 'philosophical hero' of all-time.

Drawing on one of the ancient Greeks' central values, *competition* (see Hall 2015), philosophy is not harmed – in fact, it will be *improved* – if we include an element of 'Socratic competition'; what you might call 'healthy competition' rather than 'win-at-all-costs' competition – the aim of the Sophists, which is in contrast to dialectical philosophy's aim of discovering or moving towards the truth. And it is in this way that Socrates is acquitted of the accusation that he was just another Sophist, albeit one that didn't take any money.

Speaking of Sophists, though Heraclitus gave the world the dialectical question that is so central to philosophy – a question-type that invites, by its very nature multiple views (McCabe 2006, 2015) – it was Protagoras who explicitly *relativised* it, being the first person (recorded) to have said,

'There are always two sides to every question, opposed to each other'.[2] (See page 26 of Vol. 2 for more on Protagoras's relativism.) So, as is shown on page 20 , *dialectic* is marked by a logical dimension that ostensibly presents (at least) two sides to a problem, 'yes'/'no', 'true'/'false', that demands unpacking and resolution (McCabe 2006, 2015). But Protagoras goes one step further by suggesting that it can *never* be resolved, that there is *always* more than one side because there are *always* different points of view. (See pages 25–27 of Vol. 2.)

Competition, and the investment in an idea (see page 24 of Vol. 2) this can bring about, may help to protect philosophical enquiries from collapsing into this extreme global relativism, from becoming bland exchanges of opinion where nobody is particularly invested in any one view or position, where there's always another side to the coin. A little competition may thereby preserve the notion that, certainly from an *evaluativist* point of view, some ideas are better than others (i.e., better reasoned), because, no matter how much we may prefer to say that 'all ideas are equal', they are not. Of course, all ideas are equally welcome (deliberately offensive comments aside), and deserve equal consideration, but not all ideas are logically valid, or successfully support or refute what the speaker set out to support or refute.

Some of the best exchanges I've witnessed in philosophy sessions in schools are those where two pupils 'lock horns' competitively, but in an appropriate way: they are respectful, they respond explicitly to the challenges made, they are not going to back down easily, but they will when they are shown that there's good reason to do so. They might even back down, continue thinking about it and then offer their retort later. And sometimes the retort is a good one, and one that was arrived at by a spirit of competition, through a need to prove oneself. Collaboration is good, and should be sought in a philosophical enquiry, but competition can push one to greater heights where (certainly *uncritical*) collaboration may be content, even complacent.

So, does competition have a role in philosophical enquiries in schools? Well, if we learn anything valuable about doing philosophy from Socrates it is this: *how to compete towards wisdom without (quite) becoming a Sophist.*

[1]See note 2 on page 79.
[2]The Lives of The Eminent Philosophers by Diogenes Laertius (Miller 2018).

Oracy (Articulacy)

It wasn't just that the Greeks *liked* to talk (and they did!), but, according to Hall (2015), it was the sophistication of their language that enabled them to develop their ideas as far as they did (see page 36). They also began to systematise how to best use their language by developing the arts of rhetoric, poetry and, of course, dialectical philosophy. Aristotle even kick-started the articulation of the science of logic, which many philosophers (though not all) think underpins thought and language, their use and how we understand and evaluate them both.

The Greeks stood at an important time of change in terms of language development. They had come from an oral (and therefore aural) tradition, but they were moving into a new written epoch. This tension is best caught in Plato's *Phaedrus*[16] dialogue in which Socrates says – in a written book, of course – that philosophy cannot be done properly in writing because the words are fixed, they cannot respond to objections, qualify or clarify. He thought that philosophy can only really be done through living, breathing conversations between people. PhiE is a dialectical approach to doing philosophy that is dynamic and so is, in some way, organic. Philosophy grows and unfolds.

Children can go so much further through a conversation over which they have some *ownership* (see page 66) than they ever could with only the study of written words or through writing exercises. As Socrates might say, understanding travels closely with talk (see page 2). But, here we come to one of the paradoxes of philosophy that is keenly felt in the dialogues of Plato.

In the *Laches* dialogue Socrates asks, somewhat tentatively, 'And what we know, we must, I suppose, be able to state?', to which Laches replies, 'Of course' (190c). But as the dialogues, and particularly the *aporia* ('perplexity' – see page 38 of Vol. 2) of his interlocutors show, it is clearly stating what is felt or intuited (see page 60) to be the case that proves to be so difficult. One of the key features of the philosophy we get from the Greeks is the constant negotiation, the shifting shoreline, of that which can be said and that which cannot.

Oracy is not only about having a voice – and, for sure, PhiE is one effective way that Pupil Voice[17] may be given expression – it is also about understanding that there is a corresponding responsibility that comes with having a voice. We hear a great deal about the right to be heard in democracy but we hear far less about the responsibilities and duties that are necessarily implied by this right. Very basically (with the *dialectical triangle* in mind – see page 2 of Vol. 2) if I have a *right* to be heard, then I have a *duty* to listen. But it must also be the case that if I have a right to put forward my ideas, then I must be held accountable for those ideas, and my duty, then, is to be *ready to be held to account* and to be *ready to provide an account*.

Michaels and Resnick (2008) outline the conditions for 'accountable talk' as having three components:

- *Accountability to the community*
- *Accountability to reason*
- *Accountability to knowledge*

In a classroom, this may be nothing more than being asked to say *why* one thinks what one thinks, with deference to good evaluation criteria, but it may also be achieved by gently ensuring that an objection is not overlooked but responded to (see pages 63–64 of Vol. 2) after careful consideration. These demands may lead to some discomfort, but *permissible – perhaps necessary – discomfort* according to PhiE (see page 35 of Vol. 2).

Oracy: Aoidos

Though this is hardly unique to the ancient Greeks, for reasons of consistency, I shall talk about the tradition of storytelling through the ancient Greek oral tradition of *aoidos*: the singer of stories, of which Homer is one of the best-known examples. And despite Plato's hostility to the use of stories for teaching (*Republic*, book X), he used stories constantly, to teach, to provoke and to illustrate (see page 12 of Vol. 2).

Stories and storytelling stand at the heart of PhiE in a number of ways. First of all, if you take a look at *The Philosophy Foundation* resources (see pages xvii–xviii), you will notice that many of the session-plans focus around stories, either short scenarios that function like thought-experiments, or more fully fledged narratives such as a philosophically emphasised re-telling of Homer's Odyssey (see *The If Odyssey* 2012), Asimov's *Robot* stories ('The Ceebie Stories' in *The If Machine* 2011, 2019b, pp. 177–210) or the adventures of 'Sindbad the Sailor' from the *1001 Arabian Nights* (see *Once Upon an If* 2014, pp. 180–205).

The use of stories like these helps to engage the pupils, but it also helps to provide a 'concrete' context to situate the question or problem for the pupils without having to ask the pupils to offer up their own personal real-life examples for scrutiny, judgement and examination, as per the Nelsonian Socratic tradition.

Students respond so much better to stories that are told than to ones that are read, so, though it is not essential to learn to become a fully fledged ancient Greek storyteller, complete with lyre and song, learning to 'tell' your stories well is one of the best tools you could hope for to engage (socially, emotionally and intellectually), or even to *enchant* your audience (who will also be your PhiE participants!)

Elaborating on the *if-ing* idea that is also central to PhiE (see page 55 of Vol. 2), stories enable facilitators to present situations and persons *as if* they were real or true, and, as with thought-experiments, so that the participants are able to consider something under a certain set of conditions and circumstances. The better the storytelling, the easier it is for an audience to 'enter into' the representation.

Stories can help pupils approach dilemmas *as dilemmas*. So, rather than merely answering, in answer to a dilemma, 'There are reasons on both sides', stories enable the facilitator to appropriately 're-tooth' a dilemma (Worley 2014) by asking the pupil to imagine answering from the point of view of the character facing the dilemma: 'So, imagine you are Odysseus: you are the captain of a ship and now you have to make a decision about whether to tell the men about Scylla or not. What will you do, and why?' (See *The If Odyssey* and *Once Upon an If* for more on stories and storytelling in PhiE. There is also a free downloadable storytelling resource available from TPF's website called 'Sheherazad's Handbook'.)

Oracy: Small 'd' and Big 'D' Dialectics

I would add one last feature the Greeks gave the world that underpins PhiE that is worth singling out: *dialectic*, (as well as *Dialectic*). The capital 'D' *dialectic* refers to the systematic, question-and-answer inquiry approach that is developed by philosophers from Heraclitus to Hegel and beyond (see pages 12–26); it has a technical sense. However, the small 'd' dialectic' is more general and less technical (see page 22 for more on big 'D' and small 'd' dialectics). It is a two-way relationship between the people (or *demos*) and Greek society/culture.

In his *Open University* television programme, *The Greatest Show on Earth*, Dr Michael Scott makes a case for a close relationship between the development of theatre and democracy, explaining how the Greek playwrights didn't write merely to entertain but also to satirise,[18] to warn, and chiefly to raise questions with their audience thereby critically engaging their audiences with the subject matter of the plays and, by extension, their society and culture. He contrasts this with the much more propagandist aims of Roman theatre.

Plato described Athens – and he did not mean it complimentarily – as a 'theatocracy' (*Laws III* 701a), where theatre was 'the starting point of everyone's conviction that he was an authority on everything' (ibid.). This has a contemporary resonance to it: 'Everyone's a critic!'; you could also imagine someone saying something like this about social media and television.

Plato's worries about democracy notwithstanding, this dialectical relationship can be seen in many areas of Greek culture: theatre, politics, philosophy and literature. It is for this reason that Greek myths work so well as starting points for doing philosophy. They do not *preach* so much as *present* and *problematise*. In fact, this author has written a book on how to approach philosophy through the stories of the *Odyssey*, joining the ranks of others such as Plotinus and Porphyry in seeing Homer's classic as a tool for teaching philosophy, and *The Philosophy Foundation*'s David Birch has used many Greek myths in his book *Provocations: Philosophy for Secondary Schools* (Crown House 2014).

Ironically, it is these very dialectical qualities of Homer and the canon of Greek myths – that Plato objected to in his *Republic,* banning them from his curriculum – that PhiE exploits.

IN SUMMARY

In summary, drawing upon the values of the ancient Greeks, we find that PhiE is exploratory as well as justificatory – more than welcoming – it actively *promotes* dissent as well as the autonomy of the individuals within the PhiE community. However, being part of a community, this dissenting, individualistic aspect is tempered by the nature of group inquiry, a relationship of inclusion and collaboration between different individuals, or 'friendship' in a special, qualified sense. Excellence – not elitism – is celebrated, aimed for and utilised within a PhiE to ensure that it does not collapse into a bland sharing of opinions and stories, while a careful eye is kept on the subtle difference between the 'philosophical dogs and tyrannical wolves', to borrow a phrase from Cinzia Arruzza (2016). PhiE, and philosophy more generally, is not just about thinking, it's about articulating one's thoughts, experiences, feelings and intuitions and so PhiE must provide the optimum conditions for articulation to occur, not merely to be possible.

NOTES

1. https://www.gov.uk/education/spiritual-moral-social-and-cultural-devel opment.
2. https://www.gov.uk/government/publications/prevent-duty-guidance.
3. See my Tedx talk 'Collaboration: How to be a rebel'.
4. Tedx Talk for King's College School, 'How to be a rebel': https://www.you tube.com/watch?v=53h13aPcVw0.
5. Thank you to Miriam Cohen Christofidis for this insight about self-appeal.
6. See page xxx for my translation choice.
7. Thanks to Mark Vernon's online talk 'Philosophy as awakening' and his analysis of Owen Barfield for some of the insights in this section: https://www.you tube.com/watch?v=IUbCXAYBm4o and https://www.youtube.com/watch?v=ayv EUtq_bTQ&t=5s.
8. When I use the spelling 'inquiry' it is used in the everyday sense of the word; when I use 'enquiry' it refers to the specific process of a philosophical enquiry with a group of people. See page 26 for more on the spelling/conceptual differences.
9. That can be viewed from the link on pages xvii–xviii.
10. See Nietzsche's *The Birth of Tragedy* (1999). See also page 8.

11. See also Xenophon's 'Socratic' *Symposium* (1990) and other works about Socrates, providing us with the only other extensive, surviving, contemporary account of Socrates to Plato's. It is fascinating to observe the similarities and differences between the two accounts, what it may say about Socrates but also what it may say about the two writers.

12. Not to be confused with *xenophilia*, which has a sexual meaning.

13. What Eastop, Eastop and Hartley have coined a 'difference exchange': http://www.differenceexchange.com/about.htm.

14. Nicely encapsulated in the poem by Muhammad Ali:

Me

We

15. See Plato's Apology (20e–21a).

16. See 'The Myth of Thoth and Thamus' by Clare Field in *The Philosophy Shop* (ed. P. Worley 2012) for a lesson plan around the tensions between the oral and written traditions.

17. *Pupil Voice* is an educational initiative designed to include pupils in decisions that affect their welfare.

18. Well-known characters in Athens were often satirised in plays. See Aristophanes' *The Clouds* (2003) for a satirical portrait of Socrates.

Part Three

Pedagogical Principles of PhiE

Having explained how philosophy is understood in PhiE, what is meant by dialectic and having outlined PhiE's core values, what follows is an explanation of the principles and assumptions that underlie the classroom practice.

A SENSITIVE METHOD

The first assumption is that *children can do philosophy*. At odds with Plato, who thought that it was not proper for younger people to do philosophy (see page 53 below), the 18th-century English philosopher John Locke said that children are capable of rational discussion 'by such reasons as their age and understanding are capable of' and with 'few and plain words' (1996). In his essay, 'Some thoughts concerning education and of the conduct of the understanding', he challenged contemporary views of childhood by considering children as rational creatures at a time when children were expected to be 'seen and not heard'.

Since then, traditional notions of childhood have been challenged a good deal more. Central to the practice of doing philosophy in schools is the belief that children are sufficiently rational, reflective and creative to be able to participate in philosophical conversations in two important senses: with the necessary *capability* to do so (with qualification – see below), and with sufficient *interest* to have the *desire* to do so.

I will not question this assumption, as my near-twenty-years' experience shows the claim *that children can do philosophy* to be indubitably true: they can – to varying extents of ability and success – reason ('I think . . . because . . .'), they can make inferences ('If . . . then . . .'), they can see what is wrong with faulty inferences ('Just because . . . doesn't necessarily mean . . .'), and

51

in addition to these basic moves, they can provide counterexamples to general claims, they can create thought-experiments, they can introspect, they can conceptualise, they can abstract, they can wonder and speculate, they can re-evaluate, they can draw distinctions, they can follow implications, they can entertain an idea without accepting it and so on and so forth.

But there are limits – that again vary from child to child – to how far children can go when doing philosophy. For instance, there are points at which they get lost, disengage or start to sound contradictory. It should be noted that adults, too, reach these points when doing philosophy.

PhiE is a method that is designed to be sensitive to these facts. Though PhiE sometimes takes the children – and adults – to their philosophical and conceptual limits, it does not expect from the participants what they cannot do, its *descriptive* (see below) underpinning – that is: the content of the discussion coming largely from the children themselves, from what they can *in fact* do – means that it remains sensitive to their abilities and limitations and that PhiE's parameters also change with their changing abilities and limitations. If doing philosophy through a PhiE does take someone to their conceptual limits, then it can be considered a success for doing so.

This descriptive aspect is an important difference between PhiE and academic, university philosophy where students are expected (prescriptively) to attain a certain level of knowledge, understanding and expertise for which they will *in some way* be tested; in academic philosophy there is a greater prescriptive expectation.

A DESCRIPTIVE APPROACH

This 'descriptive' approach is an approach to teaching based on what pupils *in fact do*. This contrasts with a 'prescriptive' approach which is based on what they *should* do or are expected to do. So, if you are teaching formal argumentation to sixteen-year-olds and you were approaching this *prescriptively* you would show slides of what arguments are, what a good argument is and then provide some examples for them to identify and evaluate. Only then will they be asked to have a go themselves. A teacher using the descriptive approach waits for someone to construct an argument, which is something the pupils do every time they say, 'I think . . . because . . .' (see page 98 of Vol. 2), and then the teacher uses the arguments that have been used by the pupils to teach what arguments are. This may involve several stages: *highlighting* and *labelling, teaching, consolidating, applying and strategising* (see page 94 of Vol. 2 for more on this).

This method can be used to teach critical thinking skills (see pages 94–105 of Vol. 2) because children begin using certain critical thinking skills (see pages 51–52 and 70 of Vol. 1 and 98 of Vol. 2) from a young age, naturally and intuitively without having to be taught them. Questioning and writing can be taught this way, too. The Sibelius Model (see page 87 of Vol. 2), an approach to teaching curriculum content within a PhiE, has a descriptive element to it because it encourages pupils to descriptively anticipate ideas through discussion that are part of the prescribed course.

PHILOSOPHICAL MATURITY: WAS PLATO WRONG?

In his book, *Plato Was Wrong!* David Shapiro (2012) declares that – you guessed it! – 'Plato was wrong!' Then he goes on to say that Plato was wrong *about* 'the age at which a person should start doing philosophy.' Plato has Socrates say in *Republic* Bk VII, '. . . when young people get their first taste of arguments, they misuse it by treating it as a kind of game of contradiction. They imitate those who've refuted them by refuting others themselves, and, like puppies, they enjoy dragging and tearing those around them with their arguments' (539a-b). Then, a little later, he says, 'But an older person won't want to take part in such madness. He'll imitate someone who is willing to engage in discussion in order to look for the truth' (539c).

Plato *was* wrong about this in that he conflated *stage* with *age*. Yes, some children will treat arguments 'like puppies', resorting to sophistic (see page 42) tricks to win the argument (though, often unaware that this is what they are doing), but cognitive development is much more fluid than that. Anecdotally, I have seen many primary-aged children accord with the second of the two profiles and I've seen plenty of older pupils and adults who accord with the former. Sometimes, I've seen pupils become less mature, in this respect, as they enter their teens than they were at age nine or ten.

Regarding the view that children below a certain age cannot abstract, I've seen children as young as five abstract perfectly well, and I've met plenty of adults who struggle to do so. But Plato was *right*, in that he identified an important distinction between, what we might call, *philosophical immaturity* and *maturity*: something like, respectively, the difference between self-serving sophistry and serving truth, understanding and wisdom. PhiE aims to model the second of these from a young age and does not automatically assume that one's philosophical development aligns with one's age. (See below for researchers that support this view.)

It's appropriate that Plato refers to young people doing philosophy as 'puppies' because in the *Sophist* dialogue he describes the difference between sophistry and philosophy or 'noble sophistry' (see page 42) as the difference between wolves and dogs. The difference, then, between the sophistry of young children and that of adults is a maturity and therefore a knowingness. Children do sometimes use 'tricks', such as an *equivocation* – a slippage between different meanings of a word – without knowing that it is a fallacy, whereas the adult Sophist knows full well that they are exploiting a fallacy but continue to use it if it suits their purposes.

CAPABILITY

It is no good attempting to do philosophy with a cat even though, presumably, cats can reason. This is because the cat will never make the necessary linguistic developments to apply its reason to doing something like philosophy. The practice of philosophy is therefore not only about thinking but, necessarily, also about the expression and articulation of thoughts (see page 65 and Oracy on page 44).

Neither can a new-born baby do philosophy, but the difference is that the new-born baby will, unlike the cat, develop its cognitive faculties and language skills such that he or she will one day be able to philosophise, special educational needs and exceptional circumstances such as brain-damage notwithstanding. Even in these circumstances, there may still be an extent to which philosophy can be done or approached (see Cassidy et al. 2018).

Generally speaking, from my own experiences and observations, most children are developed enough to be able to begin, in a qualified way, engaging in philosophical thinking somewhere between the ages of five and seven. This is supported by research (Matthews 1980; Astington 1993; Gopnik et al. 1999; and Gopnik 2009 – see Appendix 1 on page 81 for more on PhiE's links to research). The question now, then, is not 'Can children do philosophy?' but, 'To what extent can they do philosophy and how might it differ from adult philosophy?' then, 'What are the best ways to get children doing philosophy?' and, 'Are there ways to optimise their doing philosophy?' This book assumes that children can do philosophy and aims to answer these further questions.

At TPF, we also work with younger children between the ages of three and six years, but we do not claim that what these children do is *philosophy proper*, and, by this, I mean they are not able to employ enough of the sorts of thinking skills and moves listed above (see pages 51–52) for philosophy to begin to emerge. We do, however, describe what we do with this age group as *pre-philosophical*: preparing them with the basic format, tools and vocabulary to be able to begin doing dialectical philosophy when they are old enough, and this may be at different ages for different children.

Of all the approaches to doing philosophy with very young children, the closed-questioning approach of PhiE (see page 46 of Vol. 2) works well.[1] Though pre-school children are not able to formulate, sort between or vote on questions as per the 10 Step Model (see note 2 on page 34) – most do not know what a question is, after all – some of them can *meaningfully answer* a question with a 'yes' or a 'no'. Sometimes they can *provide a reason*, too, and on rare occasions, they can demonstrate the beginnings of *critical engagement* (see page 4 of Vol. 2) that go beyond merely saying 'yes' or 'no' and providing a reason: e.g., 'I disagree with . . . because . . .'.

The following are the basic salient requirements of being able to begin doing dialectical philosophy (and why a cat cannot!): a) to *meaningfully answer a question in thought, and attempt to articulate it verbally*, b) to *make inferences*, c) to *provide a verbal reason or reasons* and d) to *evaluate answers and reasons to questions*.

Pre-philosophy programmes, which work towards these criteria, should be understood holistically as part of a wider programme of doing philosophy from the age of 3 and ending at 11, or, even better, 16. An instrumental music teacher, or similarly inclined parent, may well begin by teaching a child music from a very young age, but, though the overall aim is to play a particular instrument, they may well not pick up the instrument for as long as a year. The child is prepared by clapping, singing, dancing and playing games; all highly valuable activities for the child in preparation for playing an instrument, as well as being valuable – and enjoyable – in and of themselves.

INTEREST AND ENGAGEMENT

'You can lead a horse to water, but you can't make it *think*', as the saying *nearly* goes. Likewise, with children, you can provide optimal conditions for doing philosophy, but you can't *force* philosophy to happen; as Plato says in *Republic* (536e), '. . . nothing taught by force stays in the soul'. In this book, you will learn how to set optimal conditions (see page 57); after that, all you can do is *invite* the children to respond and to think together (see page 3 of Vol. 2). It is however, extremely rare that, once the right conditions have been properly established, the class does not respond in a way that can become philosophical (see the procedural conduciveness on page 7 of Vol. 2). And, where this does fail to happen, it is usually because of some deeper reasons within the class.

I was originally intrigued by the idea of doing philosophy with children by observing the 'ensemble effect' in my music lessons (see page xxi): where a group may attain something greater than an individual is able to. It is true that, on the whole, groups of children are able to sustain philosophy for much longer than an individual child, and the main reason for this is that a group is able to provide a sufficient *diversity of ideas* and *range of abilities* to keep things moving and to sustain interest over a long period of time; a standard PhiE session is usually forty-five minutes to an hour long for anywhere between eight to thirty children aged 6 and upwards.

THE NEED FOR CONDITIONS

If you were to ask a philosophical question to a group of children and then walk away and leave them to discuss it, apart from a few rare exceptions, the discussion wouldn't get very far. There's a number of possible reasons for this: it is likely that they wouldn't have the wherewithal to manage the discussion so that they may all listen to each other; there would quickly become dominant speakers; they wouldn't have a lot more to say than their first thought or two, and they would become easily distracted, either, away from the philosophical aspect of the conversation, or from any kind of conversation at all!

When I ask my daughter (aged eight at the time of writing) philosophical questions, she may respond for a short while, but will quickly lose interest. Sometimes she says, 'Daddy, stop doing philosophy on me!' These failures of philosophy to be sustained are because the conditions are not right for philosophy at that particular time and in that particular context. This does not mean, however, that children can't do philosophy; *under the right conditions* they *can* do philosophy and can, *under the right conditions*, do it well.

Conversely, although higher numbers of children can sustain philosophy for longer than a single child usually can, too many children (more than thirty) will often mean that they have to wait so long to speak that they will lose interest and start to disengage.

Children do wonder and Plato famously said that 'this [wonder] is where philosophy begins'[2] (*Theaetetus* 155d) and it is sometimes inferred from this that because children naturally wonder about things, they are, therefore, 'natural philosophers'. If by *wonder* we mean a 'wondering interest' then it is certainly a necessary condition: for children to be able to do philosophy, they need to be interested (see pages 21 and 55), and it is to their own natural wonderment that we might appeal to spark an interest in whatever it is we are inviting them to consider. But if we look more carefully, we see that Plato said only that philosophy *begins* in wonder.

Wonder is not sufficient for child philosophers: wonderment does not, in and of itself, make them philosophers; there are all kinds of ways that one can wonder that is non-philosophical. Something else is needed to have that wonderment *become* philosophical. This is where the facilitator comes in. The facilitator provides the conditions for philosophy to be able to come from wonder. (See also page 28 of Vol. 2.)

In *Republic* Book VII (536e), Socrates says, '. . . don't use force to train the children . . . use *play* instead'. The first important consideration to draw philosophy from wonder, is to approach doing philosophy with a sense of *playfulness* (see page 37). So, as well as inviting the participants to enjoy themselves and to have fun *together*, they should also begin doing philosophy with a sense of spontaneity , curiosity and experimentation. I am happy to report that most of the children I work with and have worked with over the past nearly twenty years *do* enjoy it.

However, not *all* children enjoy philosophy, for a variety of reasons. I have seen classroom rules – and even rules for philosophy – that include 'Have fun!' This is well-intentioned but ill-judged as you cannot enforce fun. Whether the children enjoy doing philosophy or not is less important than whether they are *engaged*, vocally or silently, as children can be fully engaged while only thinking and listening. *Engagement*, which comes from interest and desire (see pages 21 and 55), is the *sine qua non*[3] of being able to do philosophy with children; because of the high intellectual demands philosophy makes it simply can't be done without it. Philosophy begins in wonder, and, as Plato adds, 'and nowhere else'.

Furthermore, it is *(almost)* impossible to fail to engage with a philosophical problem or question once it has been seen and understood *as* a problem, or, as Aristotle would have it, once one has seen that there is a 'knot' that needs to be untied (see page 9). But again, for this to happen, the conditions must be right.

THE CONDITIONS

What are the right conditions for PhiE? First of all, here are the optimal *environmental conditions,* and though it is not always possible to meet all these in the real world, it is good to know what they are in order to aim towards them or to fix any problems one may be having that might be because of a failure to meet these conditions:

- Low noise levels.
- No interruptions.
- Good lighting and blinds for glaring sun through windows.
- Appropriate temperature.
- The right seating (usually a format that allows for eye contact is best, such as a horse-shoe shape – see pages xxiii–xxiv of Vol. 2).
- No mobile phones or other distracting electronic devices.
- Access to resources (e.g., a board, mini-whiteboards/scrap-paper, plus the correct pens and so on - see page xxiv of Vol. 2).
- Adults in the room should be (and look like they are) listening and supportive (see pages 38, 42 and 55).
- The right classroom culture (see pages 38, 42 and 55 of Vol. 1 and 65–66 of Vol. 2).

- To have all children present for the duration of the session, where possible.
- If the facilitator is an outside provider, then the classroom teacher should be present for the duration of the session.
- There should be a disciplinary system that the facilitator and the participants are aware of and can appeal to when necessary (see TPF's blog for more on classroom management considerations).

You will notice that small things, often things you cannot control, affect the quality of sessions, such as whether the session is in the morning or afternoon, a Monday, a Wednesday or a Friday, mid-term or end-of-term, and even the weather can affect how the pupils perform. For instance, for an average Year 6 (5th grade) class, a windy Friday afternoon on the last day of term/year when there has been no outside play (recess), with a supply (substitute) teacher may not produce the best results.

Once the environmental conditions are optimised, the *intellectual conditions* can be put in place (relate to model on page 17):

- Provide a *stimulus* and/or a *question that is likely to interest the group and that elicits a diversity of intuitions* (pre-reflective ideas).
- Have a good way of *voicing those intuitions* so that all can hear and con-sider (see Preface, Part One and 'Listen' on pages 27–33 of Vol. 2) them.
- Have a good way to *elicit* responses, reflections, reasons, evaluations and re-evaluations (see 'Open Questioning Mindset' in Vol. 1 and Part Two in Vol. 2).
- Have a good way to *elicit more* from the children so that their first (or 'surface') response is not all you may get from them (see 'Opening-up' on page 41 of Vol. 2).
- Give them *time and space to consider* the question and what they hear said in the group, for themselves, with each other, and to the group so that they may *work towards seeing philosophical problems for themselves*.
- Have ways to *structure the dialogue* so that *progress can be made* where it is possible for progress to be made (see all of Vol. 2).
- Ensure that you structure your questioning and provide the children with the necessary vocabulary so that *genuine evaluation* of claims, ideas and positions may take place (see Part Three of Vol. 2).
- Have ways to ensure that the *ideas and direction* of the discussion are, as far as possible, *the children's own*, except where curriculum content is being delivered (see pages 66–76).

Ideal Speech Situations

The conditions so far described imply what the philosopher Habermas (1990) calls an *ideal speech situation* (ISS). This is a situation where discourse occurs within optimal rational conditions, where the criteria is 'What is being claimed? What are the reasons for the claim? And are they good reasons?'; where other, usual, extraneous considerations (e.g., pupil status within the group), and non-rational, coercive influences (e.g., force or threat of force) are removed, or at least, minimised as far as possible. One of the roles of the facilitator is to make ISS conditions possible within a classroom and to maintain them as far as the facilitator is able.

Although it is possible to 'set' these conditions authoritatively (for instance, at the early stages or with very young children), it is not possible to *enforce* them in the long run; the pupils must, in the end, be *persuaded internally* (where the motivation to take part is a willing one) that doing philosophy is worthwhile and that these conditions are good conditions for dialogue contexts such as philosophy, in order for PhiE (and other approaches to doing philosophy) to work.

Acquainting them with ideas and discussions that interest them, and any ensuing good quality discussions are the best way to do this, as well as allowing them to get involved while providing them with the opportunities to do so. (See page 9 of Vol. 2 to help realise the right conditions.) The adoption of an Open Questioning Mindset (OQM – see page 71) by the facilitator is also an important way that ISS is achieved as this helps to minimise subtle and implicit ways that a facilitator may impose his or her authority, unconscious biases or status covertly onto the group.

CLASSROOM CULTURE

Internal acquiescence is best achieved through a good classroom culture and from the adoption of the right mindset by the teacher/facilitator (see page 71). The class must *trust* the teacher/facilitator (e.g., no jokes at the class's expense, sarcasm, or ridicule), they must be able to *predict* how the teacher will respond (this will happen from consistent behaviour), they must know that their teacher is *fair*, *transparent* and *honest*. The teacher can also model the right dispositions by *admitting their own errors or limits*, by showing when they have *learned from the children*, by using *tentative* language ('As far as I know . . .', 'I might be wrong but . . .', 'I was wrong about . . .') and always remaining *defeasible* (open to the possibility of being wrong).

The teacher should point them to *good sources of information*, hold the pupils *to account*, as well as be seen to be held to account themselves when necessary, explain why they have done things (punishments, rewards, speaker choices made during a session etc.). But perhaps most importantly for a facilitator of PhiE, they will often adopt and model an *OQM* (see page 74).

PHIE BEGINS WITH INTUITIONS

Key to engaging participants of a PhiE with ideas and philosophical problems quickly is activating their *intuitions*. You would be forgiven for thinking that the first and most basic 'rule' of a philosophical endeavour such as
PhiE might be: 'think!', but you may be surprised to hear that it is, in fact:
'Don't think!' or, more precisely, 'Don't think too hard, but allow your first
thoughts to come forth'.[4] Thinking comes later. This *intuitive* aspect of PhiE
corresponds to the distinction drawn by Kahneman (2011) between 'fast' and
'slow' (or 'system 1' and 'system 2') thinking, but, as with much of PhiE's
components, it has been developed and observed independently through
many years of practice through trial and error.

During my reflections at the early stages of the development of PhiE, I found
that working with a certain kind of closed question – as it would turn out,
grammatically closed but *conceptually open* (Worley 2015a) – is best for doing
philosophy (see page 14 of Vol. 2). A primary reason for this is that closed questions invite respondents to immediately *take a position* (e.g., 'yes' or 'no' – see
also pages 24 and 53 of Vol. 2), which, once opened-up (see page 41 of Vol. 2),
encourages pupils to both think and express themselves in *standard argument
form*: using *premises* and *conclusions* (see page 54 of Vol. 2). Secondly, closed
questions elicit *intuitions*, or pre-reflective positions, very naturally.

Many philosophical problems arise when we have more than one intuition
in response to a question and where those intuitions seem both *plausible* and
yet in *conflict*.[5] (See also page 24 of Vol. 2.) For example, the classic philosophical 'problem of free will' arises when we consider the question, 'Do
we have a free will?' One plausible answer to this is that we do, because it
appears to us that we choose freely, and yet another plausible answer is that
we don't, because everything, understood a certain way, seems to be subject
to determining laws and it may appear intuitive to many of us that our own
actions are also products of determining laws.

The first of these intuitions is more likely to be the pre-reflective intuition
held by most people (see the ancient Greek *doxa* on page 15 and *endoxa* on
page 25). The second requires a little more thought, clarity and structure
to one's thinking to arrive at and so is more likely to follow from a more
deliberative philosophical process. Once these intuitions have been arrived
at, there is a problem because it also seems intuitive that we can't hang on to
both these intuitions: that either we have a free will or we don't. If we hang
on to both it would appear that we have a contradiction: that we both have a
free will and that we don't have a free will (formally, a contradiction is represented like so: '*p and not-p*'. See pages 5, 7, 18, 25 and 26 for more on this
aspect of doing philosophy). So, either we have to reject one of these intuitive
positions or we need to make sense of how we could hang on to both of them.

The job of professional philosophers is to take problems like this and consider them more carefully. This will often include the basic move of deciding whether the *apparent contradiction* is a *genuine contradiction* or one that can be resolved by appeal to carefully wrought *distinctions* and clearly *defined terms*. It may turn out, for instance, that there are *different kinds* – or *different senses* – of 'free will' that might help us make sense of the apparent contradiction.

What marks a professional philosopher is her ability to respond to a question in a full sense: as well as being able to refer to what others have said in the past, she can also identify her own intuitive responses, imagine what the general intuitive response or responses are likely to be, clearly and accurately articulate those responses – often in more than one way – consider any further responses to those responses, see problems in those responses, investigate whether those problems are irresolvable, and perhaps even attempt to answer the question, usually conditionally, based upon the various (often provisional) definitions and distinctions she may have drawn.

It is a highly complex task for one mind to do all this, and most children (most adults, too!) will struggle to do all this by themselves *if they are not Aristotle or Hypatia!* But, the 'ensemble effect' (see pages xxi, 55 and 62) means that a group may be able to begin doing many of these things – and sustain them too – though they would not be able to do so on their own. So, PhiE provides a forum for a group of children (or adults) to begin structuring a dialectical approach to philosophical problems. It[6]

- asks a *grammatically closed but conceptually open question* (e.g., 'Does the future exist?') See page 14 of Vol. 2.
- *takes responses* (and reasons, where possible) to the question. (e.g., 'I think the future does/does not exist because . . .') See page 3 of Vol. 2.
- *elicits different responses* (and reasons, where possible) to the question, such as 'yes', 'no', 'both', 'neither' or 'in a way yes, and in a way no' and so on (e.g., 'Is there anyone who thinks that the future does/does not exist?' or 'Is there anyone who thinks something different to what we've heard so far?') See page 5 of Vol. 2.
- *engages* the participants with those responses and reasons ('What do you think of what's been said?') See page 4 of Vol. 2.
- *critically engages* the participants with those responses and reasons ('Is what X said right?')
- invites *re-evaluation* ('Has anyone changed their mind?' or 'So, what do you think about it now?' and so on)
- uncovers or formulates *new questions* (see page 66 of Vol. 2)
- invites the group to *consider its progress* re: answering the question or resolving the problem ('What's the best way to answer the question?' and 'How have we/you done at answering the question?') See page 94 of Vol. 2.

The beauty of PhiE's 'intuitive' approach to doing philosophy is that there are no huge intellectual demands to get things going; the children do not need to be acquainted with philosophical literature or the history of ideas, neither do they need to be able to formulate questions and understand or follow voting procedures; all the pupils need is to have an intuitive response to a question, and the only vocabulary they need to start doing this is 'yes' and 'no'.

That's all the 'kindle' needed to begin doing philosophy with children using PhiE. This means that very young children can be included in the same systematic philosophy programme as older children. Remember how simple Parmenides' conditions of dialectic are: 'You can think and you can speak' (see pages 13 of Vol. 1 and 2 of Vol. 2). PhiE works on the same principle.

In addition, what requires a good deal of thought for one may be relatively intuitive to another, such as when a Year 5 girl saw 'in a flash' that the nine times table is a palindrome (I had to write it out carefully before I saw it!). This means that a philosophical enquiry may be sustained by a series of intuitive moves from different members of the group at different times and about different things (the ensemble effect – see page xxi). So, it may well be that the role of intuition is not limited only to the beginning of an enquiry but continues to lead people up the ladder of enquiry when conducted with many people.

There is a further virtue to this that has been pointed out by my colleague Andy West (2015). He says that this closed-questioning approach 'allows children to access philosophy regardless of their *cultural currency*'. He goes on to say:

'When the teacher shows a painting to the class, they ask: what is art? When the teacher tells a story about a ship that has all its parts replaced with new ones, they ask: is it the same ship? Both are philosophical questions. The art question is more accessible to those children who have been to galleries, but the children who haven't been on a ship will still be able to discuss the themes of identity behind the ship question. Crucially, the ship question creates an inclusive classroom because it's a closed question and it requires the child to have only an intuitive yes or no reaction. It's then the philosophy teacher's job to help the child develop their response into a reasoned argument. Where responding to the art question requires the child to be articulate before answering, the ship question is designed to help children become more articulate by answering'. (*The Guardian*, Thursday 19 November 2015)

WITHIN AND WITHOUT: IS PHIE DEMOCRATIC?

The underlying dialectical – that is, 'question-and-answer' – foundation to PhiE (see Part One of Vol. 1) also shows how PhiE is, in a minimal sense, *democratic*, as democracy too shares this question-and-answer foundation (see page 47).

Beyond this minimal sense, PhiE takes a *negative* position in that, though it plays a role in instantiating democratic activity among pupils, it should not be used to overtly or covertly shape pupils beyond this basic dialectical relationship. Philosophy in the curriculum, in many countries, currently sits on the periphery: it is not part of the core curriculum and does not have a centralised syllabus imposed upon it. This means that its role in education is to be both *within and without* it.

Some argue that because any educational intervention is non-neutral it is therefore okay for educational interventions to actively and positively (that is, not merely negatively as PhiE does) promote democratic ideals. This commits the *is/ought fallacy*: that because something *is* the case (that interventions are necessarily non-neutral) it is morally permissible to actively promote a given value (such as democratic principles). For instance, just because human beings, through their actions, in some way demonstrate consumption, it does not mean that it is okay to or that they must necessarily promote *consumerism*; many 'consumers' are actively opposed to 'consumerism' being a central value of society.

When philosophy is used instrumentally like this, it sails dangerously close to becoming subsumed into social engineering programmes. There exists a tension between philosophy's aim of developing autonomous, critical thinkers and external citizenship agendas. The answer may lie in continuing to build a culture of doing philosophy in the current education systems with teachers and educators, but one which resists becoming part of any core curriculum, and therefore becoming too centralised.

TRUTH AND KNOWLEDGE

What is PhiE's epistemology, or theory of knowledge? One reason why PhiE resists the 'P4/wC' umbrella-term is that Lipman/Sharp's P4C grew out of pragmatist foundations, particularly Pierce and Dewey. It is far from unanimous, however, that P4C and P4/wC (see note 1 on page xxxiv) is committed to pragmatist assumptions, and Catherine McCall has said that McCall's CoPI is (and should be) premised on *external realist* assumptions: that there is a mind-independent world 'out there' waiting for us to discover by whatever rational means there is at our disposal (2009). McCall also thinks that some P4/wC practice, because of its pragmatist foundations, collapses the metaphysical with the epistemological; in other words, the truth *becomes* what we can or do *know* about the truth (ibid.).

So, what are PhiE's epistemological commitments or implications? On the one hand, I am reluctant to categorically claim what is the 'correct' epistemology, for the obvious reason that epistemology and epistemological justification is itself a legitimate object of philosophical enquiry, and given that PhiE is a way of doing philosophy, it might not want to presume something so contentious about its own method and objects of enquiry. And one thing we learn from Socrates, Plato and Aristotle is that philosophy itself should not be overlooked as a legitimate object of philosophical inquiry.

On the other hand, PhiE is a method committed to the development of *intellectual virtues/excellences,* or, those attributes, dispositions and attitudes that help participants become better 'knowers' or better 'understanders'. In this way, philosophy has a paradox at its heart: it is a questioning enterprise into which everything (including itself) falls within its questioning purview, but it needs to assume tools with which to question so as not to be rendered useless or absurd. In true Heraclitean spirit (see 'The unity of opposites' on pages 5 and 36), we should not let a paradox deter us (compare this with Plato's 'paradox of inquiry' in his *Meno* dialogue).

Though Socrates and Plato worked to essentialist/realist assumptions, having Socrates and Plato as main sources of inspiration does not commit PhiE to *essentialism* or *realism* (see pages 19 and 20); Socratic/Platonic method stands apart from the intellectual assumptions of the day in that there can be great value in pursuing Socratic ends even if one does not share his belief that an exhaustive list of necessary and sufficient conditions is possible, or even necessary.

Through the *elenctic* process (see page 17), one may arrive at a richer, more nuanced, better-understood notion of X, without having fully defined X, or without a full definition even being possible. In practice, Plato was committed to *defeasibility* (the view that one may be in error). We see this in his own re-evaluative process: his robust cases for the Forms in *Republic* and *Phaedo* for example, matched by his equally robust critique of the same theory, especially in *Parmenides*.

The message from the dialogues is that philosophy is not concluded or 'enclosed' in one all-encompassing theory, but something that is ongoing and continuous, something Plato invites his readers to engage with and embark on, just as the best models of his characters do, notably, Socrates.

Similarly, PhiE sees philosophy as 'non-enclosed' and so suspends any strong epistemological commitments on the basis that these should be considered legitimate candidate objects of a PhiE investigation; there is, therefore, a kind of *epistemological suspension*. While, at the same time, there are some necessary provisional 'working assumptions'. Here are some suggested, provisional epistemological assumptions of PhiE:

- One can have pre-reflective intuitions about something (it is **intuitive**)
- One can attempt to *articulate* those intuitions (it is **expressive**)
- One can have *reasons* in support of – or against – one's intuitions (it is **rational**)
- One can attempt to clearly *articulate* and *formulate* any reasons one might have or that there might be (it is **articulative**)
- There will be opportunities to *re-articulate* and *re-formulate* when necessary (it is **dynamic**)
- There is an assumed structure of justification based on *reliable inference-making processes*, or, good reasoning that is ordinarily comprehensible to non-specialists (it is **reliabalist** and **inclusive**)
- *Doubt* should be applied to claims and beliefs, and claims and beliefs should be accepted only *provisionally* (it is **fallibilist**; not in the strong sense that *no truth can ever be achieved*, but in the weaker sense of an intellectual virtue or disposition that it is *a good general rule to apply doubt to a claim that has been presented*)
- There is an expectation that one bases *judgements* on the *best reasons available* (it is **judgement-making-oriented** and **normative**. *Judgement-making-oriented* is to be distinguished from *judgementalism:* prejudging without sufficient information.)
- There is an assumption that one may be right or wrong (where the notions of right and wrong are appropriate), consistent or inconsistent, coherent or incoherent, cogent or non-cogent (it is **evaluative**)
- There is always the opportunity to put *into question* (see note 7 on page 80 and page 67 of Vol. 2) any of these assumptions, intuitions, reasons, or judgements made during a PhiE on the basis of good reasons (it is **re-evaluative**)

Following McCabe's claim that dialectic's emphasis is exploratory rather than about 'getting the right answer' (McCabe 2015 – see page 14), PhiE is, among many other things, also a process of *encountering, discovering* and *explaining* one's own epistemology, having this implicitly and explicitly challenged by the group through the process of doing PhiE. This is in contrast to aiming towards an overarching, epistemological standard such as pragmatism, external realism and so on.

One may well have a different, implicit epistemological outlook at one time than at another or at one stage of one's development than at another, and there may well be a variety of different implicit epistemological working assumptions among the members of one class or group (Kuhn and Dean 2004 – see page 25 of Vol. 2). It may even be that one improves and refines one's own operational epistemological outlook/mechanism by doing PhiE (see 'Metacognition' on pages 94 and especially 109 of Vol. 2), or it may be that this develops alongside it, independently of it.

(See also pages 11, 33 and 37 of Vol. 1 and 18, 24–26, 35–36, 82 and 107 of Vol. 2 on the issue of 'no right and wrong answers', and page 95 of Vol. 2 for a ten-year-old taking an explicit epistemological attitude in PhiE.)

OWNERSHIP

If your child does not eat vegetables, there is a simple way to help encourage him or her to be more open to eating them that is often taught by child behaviour experts: have regular 'pizza-making days'. By having your child make a pizza, top it and then cook it, they take ownership of the pizza and, being more invested, are more likely to eat it all, including the vegetables they placed on top themselves. I've seen this work! The same principle is at work when doing philosophy with children. By *ownership* I mean that the children need to:

- know why they are saying what they are saying (e.g., what question what they are saying answers, and why it might matter; what role it plays in the discussion);
- say what they think and not what the teacher wants them to say, or what they *think* the teacher wants them to say (see page 71);
- decide for themselves, perhaps with some coaching and guidance, how to progress in the discussion (see page 84 of Vol. 2);
- make mistakes, misunderstand one another, get lost and experience *aporia* (see page 38 of Vol. 2);
- be confused or perplexed for the right reasons (see distinction between *present* and *absent* confusion/ignorance on page 38 of Vol. 2); and
- take responsibility for things they say and therefore be held accountable (see pages 45 of Vol. 1 and 63–64 of Vol. 2).

It is not essential in order for them to have ownership that they choose the question or the topic of consideration, but it is essential that the way any ensuing discussion follows a question be, to as great an extent as possible, a result of the group's own 'direction-making'. This is complex, as a group of people involved in a philosophical discussion is (are?!) not a single entity, though the members of the group are, in some way, working together to consider a question and towards progress with regards answering it.

TWO KEYSTONE PRINCIPLES IN PHIE: ABSENCE AND OPEN QUESTIONING MINDSET

Absence and Presence

Now we come to the two central, keystone ideas in PhiE that are themselves closely related, and that help to ensure both ownership and autonomy are maintained and preserved within PhiE. It is essential that you have a good grasp of these two principles before attempting to practice PhiE in the classroom. The principles are *absence* (this section) and *OQM* (the next section). First, *absence*.

This section begins with a story that has its origins in a civilisation that precedes even the ancient Greeks: what we know as the 'Minoan' empire, the power-base of which was the island we now call Crete. In the ancient Greek myth, Theseus, the son of king Aegeus of Athens, is selected, together with thirteen other youths of Athens (seven boys and seven girls), to travel to the island of Minoa (modern Crete) for sacrifice. They are to be offered to Asterion, or the 'Minotaur', a half-man-half-bull monster imprisoned in a labyrinth built by the master craftsman Daedalus.

Before the youths are sent to their deaths, Theseus and Ariadne, the daughter of Minos and half-sister to the Minotaur, fall in love. She goes to see Daedalus for help and he gives her a ball of thread that she in turn gives to Theseus to help him (in some versions) find his way *to* the Minotaur and (in all versions) to find his way out of the labyrinth, once he has killed the beast. His defeat of the Minotaur frees the Athenians from this terrible tribute demanded, annually, by King Minos.

There are some useful parallels to be found in this myth between the story and the facilitation of PhiE. Theseus can be seen to stand in for the *participants* involved in a philosophical enquiry, the labyrinth stands for *philosophy* itself (or, more broadly, any form of complex thinking), the Minotaur could stand in for the *problem* (or that which the group is trying to resolve in some way). Finally, and most significantly from the point of view of the facilitation of a philosophical enquiry, Ariadne stands in for the *facilitator*.

The emblematic figure of Ariadne affords two important features of facilitation: she provides Theseus with a ball of thread to help him *navigate* his way through the labyrinth, but – crucially – she is not with him while he is in the labyrinth; her help, therefore, is offered at something of a distance from him and his engagement with the problem he is faced with . These two notions, of 'helping' but 'at a distance', can be nicely captured in the words *presence* and *absence* (Worley 2016).

By *presence* I mean interventions made by the facilitator that impact, in some way, on the group's progress (e.g., asking a question, or having the group take part in an activity of some kind), and by *absence* I mean any intentional refraining from making an intervention (e.g., the decision not to ask a question or introduce an activity), and the non-participation of the facilitator regarding any content (see page 1 of Vol. 2). The art of the facilitator in PhiE lies in aiming to achieve the right balance between his or her *effective presence* and *effective absence* during their facilitation of a philosophical enquiry.

In some versions of the story the thread is not magic and is unthreaded by a wooden device known as a 'clew' (also fashioned by Daedalus); in which case, the tool represents only retrospective thinking ('re-tracing one's steps'). But, in other versions of the story, the ball of thread is magic and, not only does it help him re-trace his steps back out of the labyrinth, it also leads him directly to the Minotaur in the first place. This is apposite, because in this – the 'magic' – version, the thread represents both *forward* and *backward* thinking,[7] thinking about where the conversation has been but also where it is or might be going, and therefore representing the idea of 'synoptic view-taking', or 'seeing the conversation as a whole', during a philosophical enquiry. This is especially important when considering metacognitive thinking in philosophy (see Part Three of Vol. 2).

An example of appropriate *presence* might be the use of opening-up strategies or the introduction of a new scenario to test a claim. An example of appropriate absence might be the withholding of a paraphrase to give a pupil the opportunity to clarify for him or herself, or the decision not to comment but to simply pass the ball or open up to the group.

In his seminal piece 'On Educating Children', Montaigne says, 'It is good to make [the pupil] trot in front of his tutor in order to judge his paces and to judge how far down the tutor needs to go to adapt himself to his ability. If we get that proportion wrong', he says, 'we spoil everything; knowing how to find it and to remain well-balanced within it is one of the most arduous tasks there is' (Screech 1991).

During a PhiE, facilitators are trying to 'get that proportion right' between presence and absence, between 'stepping in' and 'stepping out' of the enquiry. Many of the techniques utilised by a PhiE facilitator are, in true Heraclitean spirit, both expressions of presence and absence simultaneously. For example, the *if-ing, anchoring and opening-up* strategies (see page 41 of Vol. 2) are examples of presence in that they are questions that are asked of the group to achieve a dialectical end, such as to elicit a reason for a taken position. At the same time, it is also an example of absence in that no content comes from the facilitator, the move is a purely structural, 'content-less' questioning move: a hinge, not a door.

SOCRATES' MIDWIFERY PRINCIPLE AND ABSENCE

Socrates famously described himself as a midwife to other people's ideas in a discussion with the character *Theaetetus* in the dialogue of the same name. He also claimed that his mother was 'a good, hefty midwife' called *Phaenarete* (which literally means 'she who brings virtue to light')[1] and that he practised what *she* practised, but by 'watch[ing] over the labour of . . . souls, not . . . bodies' (Theaetetus 150b). So, to use the Greek, Socrates and PhiE are both *maieutic*: a method of enquiry that aims to bring latent ideas into consciousness.

PhiE shares with Socrates a commitment to facilitating the bringing forth of other's ideas, and this metaphor certainly carries across to the practice of doing philosophy with children. Given PhiE's commitment to the concept of 'absence' (see above), it is particularly pertinent when Socrates says, 'The common reproach against me is that I am always asking questions of other people but never express my own views about anything' (*Theaetetus* 150c).[2] One of the distinguishing features of PhiE is that, unlike in P4/wC, the facilitators are not 'co-enquirers' (Sutcliffe and Williams 2000), but 'interested facilitators' only. In this respect, PhiE is more closely aligned with Socrates' observation here than with most other examples of his practice.

Socrates also notes how those involved in philosophical enquiries with him surprise other people and themselves with the progress they make (*Theaetetus* 150d). This is also true when people first observe an example of a PhiE in the classroom. Socrates underlines where their ideas have come from: '. . . yet this is clear this is not due to anything they have learned from me; it is that they discover within themselves a multitude of beautiful things, which they bring forth into the light'.[3] He follows this directly with, 'But it is I who deliver them of this offspring' (ibid. 150d). So, though the ideas are not his, they are brought forth because of him.

PhiE has specialised tools and techniques that help pupils bring forth their ideas (see Vol. 2), that would not have shown themselves had no facilitation occurred, but that also ensure that what is brought forth is, as much as possible, genuinely from the children (or the group). PhiE guards against – perhaps more so than Socrates – the surreptitious 'feeding' of answers to the group via suggestion and leading-questions (see pages xxxiii–xxxiv of Vol. 1 and 57–58, 42, 49 of Vol. 2), thereby realising this ideal Socratic practice that we see outlined in the midwifery metaphor in *Theaetetus*.

We also see, in the midwifery metaphor, the recurrent idea (it is also in the *Sophist* – see page 25 of Vol. 2) that philosophy is *eliminative* and oriented by its relationship to truth and knowledge. Here, Socrates talks about being on the lookout for those that give birth to 'phantom[s] and not truth' (151c). This is where the metaphor may feel a little stretched, but it does manage to convey something important about both Socrates and PhiE: that philosophy should be concerned with *evaluation* and *elimination*, not only *expression* and *exploration* (see page 25 of Vol. 2).

From Within

The maieutic idea that those engaged in enquiry 'discover within themselves a multitude of . . . things' (see above) in *Theaetetus* is taken up again in the *Meno*, this time in a fully fledged theory, the theory of *recollection* (*anamnesis*), in which he claims that learning is simply recollecting knowledge that was once before possessed but now forgotten.

We may not share Socrates' metaphysical beliefs in the immortality of the soul, but we can still accept that much of what the children do when they do philosophy is something that comes, *in a sense*, from within themselves. We see how this might be the case when we look at Socrates' proof of his theory. When Meno asks Socrates to prove this theory, Socrates invites a slave boy over to him and proceeds to question him about a geometrical problem he outlines in the sand. He asks Meno to observe how he only asks the boy questions and does not provide him with answers.

The boy does indeed eventually solve the problem and answers the question Socrates asked him at the start – at which point he couldn't answer correctly. And Socrates, arguably, does not provide him with the answers at the crucial points. What is demonstrated is the boy's ability to make *inferences*; geometry is, after all, an inference-making science, and it is this inference-making ability that children in a PhiE do not need to be taught explicitly, but that is necessary to be able to do philosophy (see pages xxviii, 7, 51, 55 of Vol. 1 and 98–100 of Vol. 2).[4]

It is in this sense that Socrates is right to say that what we need to do philosophy is 'within' us. Even as young as three, children are beginning to develop the necessary inference-making abilities that make reasoning and, therefore, philosophising possible. Because basic reasoning skills develop naturally, without being taught to them explicitly children begin to use critical thinking skills. They draw distinctions, pull on counterexamples, hypothesise, do conceptual analysis, make analogies and comparisons, show how something leads to an infinite regress, spot fallacies and much more (see pages 51–52).

[1]The correspondence between the meaning of her name and her occupation may suggest that this is a creation of Plato's.

[2]There is an interesting and tantalising parallel between Socrates' comment here and Plato himself. Plato's position of irony means that he is nowhere, in any of his extant works (with the exception of the contested seventh letter), explicitly present. Nowhere does he enter into his own voice; he only ever speaks through the mouths of others. Although Socrates' claims about absence are not always consistent with his practice, Plato remains, like Shakespeare and even more so than a PhiE facilitator, consistently hidden.

[3]Compare this phrase with Socrates' mother's name: Phaenarete. See note above.

[4]For a longer discussion of the demonstration with the slave boy in the Meno see: https://www.academia.edu/36781500/Does_the_fa mous_demonstration_with_the_slave_boy_in_Platos_Meno_prove_any thing.

Open Questioning Mindset[8]

Possibly the most important thing, before one tries facilitating his or her first PhiE, is to ensure they inhabit the right *mindset*. When we, at TPF, observe teachers and philosophers, even where the questioning is not yet quite right, and the facilitation not yet expert, if the mindset is right, a philosophical conversation will often occur by the power of the group and the basic dialectical structure (see page 2 in Vol. 2). And conversely, though the technical aspects may all be in place, if the mindset isn't right, it will be much more difficult. So, how does one get one's mindset right for facilitating PhiE?

An *OQM*, most basically expressed, is where the teacher *listens for what the participants think for themselves*. This is contrasted with a Closed Questioning Mindset (CQM) where the teacher *listens only for those ideas that the teacher wants the group or class to say*. So, the advice is: *listen, don't lead*.

Establishing an OQM in a classroom is, therefore, more a culture than a questioning move and so it can be inhabited by the questioner as well as the respondents. For instance, in the UK, a sign that CQM is in play in a classroom is when the pupils prefix answers with, 'Is it . . .?' and this is particularly telling when this happens during a philosophy session. As a litmus test, if you notice this prefix being dropped in answers given in your philosophy sessions then it is a good sign that you have established the right mindset; if you hear this prefix, then you may have some work to do.

What follows are the main features of an OQM.

Guess What's in My Head

Many readers will be familiar with the more colloquial phrase, 'Guess-what's-in-my-head' (GWIMH) teaching or questioning. A very simple example of this is as follows:

Teacher: What is the capital of France?
Pupil A: Is it Rome?
T: No. Anyone else?
B: Is it London?
T: No. Anyone else?
C: Is it Paris?
T: Yes. Well done!

GWIMH questioning is *rhetorical* in that the questioner already knows what the answer is; they are simply testing to see who else in the class knows. To this extent, it is a psychological dynamic that can be characterised as 'mind-reading': the children seek to say what the teacher is looking for or what is already in the teacher's head.

Some people are better at this 'mind-reading' dynamic than others, so, by itself, this dynamic is exclusionary. The first important characteristic of a CQM, from the point of view of the questioner, is that the questioner, when inhabiting a CQM, asks for the respondent to say *the answer the questioner is looking for*. From the point of view of the respondent, it is to *provide the answer they think the teacher is looking for* (figure 3.1).

Figure 3.1   Closed Questioning Mindset: In This Dynamic, What the Respondent Reports May Well Not Be What They Are Thinking for Themselves.

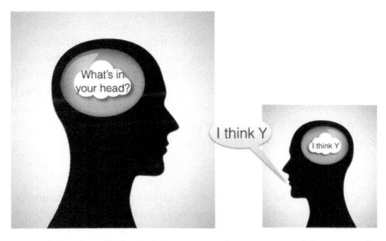

Figure 3.2 Open Questioning Mindset: Here, There Is Concord between What the Respondents Are Thinking and What They Report.

It should be pointed out that what is being recommended in this book is not that one should always be in an OQM, avoiding CQM at all times and in all teaching contexts; sometimes one *needs* to work to a *closed agenda* or *closed context* (aims and objectives, lesson-plans and so on). The key is to be *aware* of when you are in which mindset and to ask yourself: is this mindset necessary/the right one for this context? For the most part, when facilitating a PhiE, an OQM is to be preferred, but even then, there may be moments where this will not be so appropriate.

A CQM is contrasted with an OQM (see figure 3.2).

What I describe in more detail in Vol. 2 as 'the basic mechanism', *asking pupils what they think* and *why they think it* (see page 3 of Vol. 2), helps to maintain an OQM so long as you ensure that you *listen for* (see pages 27–30 of Vol. 2) what *they think* and not *what you want them to say* or *what they think you want them to say*. It's a correct instinct to try to get this aspect right that leads teachers to say, mistakenly, 'Remember, there's no right and wrong' (see page 11), but all that need be said instead is, 'I'm not looking for a particular answer; just say whatever it is you think'. Then follow this with, 'Can you say why?' (see page 41 of Vol. 2).

The best way to get this across is to demonstrate the right classroom culture (see page 58). For instance, if one responds with clear approval statements like, 'Excellent!' or 'I like that!' or 'That's a really good idea', they will very quickly pick up on what sort of thing you are looking for and try to deliver similar kinds of responses, narrowing the diversity of ideas and conferring ownership to the facilitator. These kinds of responses instantiate, often unintentionally, a CQM in the facilitator and therefore also encourage it in the participants.

Problematisation

Another feature of an OQM is the welcoming of *problematisation* – during philosophy one should *actively seek* problematisation. So, if someone asks an awkward question during a presentation you're making, or if a child spots a problem in what you're teaching that you hadn't, and if you have an OQM, you will *acknowledge* the problem and *take it seriously*. This may mean conceding, 'putting your hands up', saying that you'll have to come back to that, or putting it to the group for proper consideration.

Blocking

Blocking is when the facilitator somehow disallows problematisation or ideas into the discussion, either by inappropriately anchoring so that their new idea is side-stepped, by not opening-up (see page 41 in Vol. 2) and then just moving on or by introducing a new (or the facilitator's own) question, thereby ceasing any further thought along the participant's or group's line of enquiry.

Even when someone is saying something with contempt, to undermine the session, it is still worth, in all but a few contexts, applying an OQM rule of thumb to *take all ideas seriously and put them to the group for consideration*. Even where the speaker does not mean something seriously, the rest of the group may take it seriously, which in turn encourages the original speaker to treat their rhetorical point more seriously.

So, if possible and appropriate, say *yes* to ideas and 'let them in' for consideration.

'Guess What's In Your Head' and Intentional Sensitivity

This is important with regard to philosophical maturity on page 53 and the difference between the 'philosophical dogs and 'tyrannical, rhetorical wolves' on pages 42, 48 and 53.

Another aspect to CQM is what I call 'Guess what's in YOUR head', where the questioner constructs arguments on behalf of the participants with interpretation phrases like, 'So, what you're saying is . . .' or 'Do you mean . . .?' (see page 31 of Vol. 2 for more on paraphrasing). For instance, to take an example from page 74 of Vol. 2:

A: It's a bird, so it flies.
FAC: So, you're saying that all birds fly.

It is true to say that the statement 'It's a bird so it flies', *logically* entails the *suppressed premise* (see page 82 of Vol. 2) 'All birds fly', but there is still good reason why the facilitator should refrain from 'Guessing what's in *their* head' and saying what the facilitator thinks they mean. It is because this inference is not *psychologically* entailed (see pages 81–83 of Vol. 2 for how to use the logical entailments for furthering critical thinking).

Even though the outward expression of their thought seems to imply a logical entailment, they may not have *meant* what they said (think of Lewis Carroll's *Alice in Wonderland*, when there is a discussion about whether *saying what you mean* is the same as *meaning what you say* – and, of course, it is not the same!).

PhiE is committed to *logical* and *conceptual sensitivity*, but it is also committed to *intentional sensitivity*. And where the expression of a thought is at odds with the intention behind it, facilitators should defer to the intention over the expression. Of course, they won't necessarily know when this happens, as a facilitator will not be privy to any difference of intention, directly. So, they should question towards 'intentional excavation' (see below).

Here is a possibe meaning from the above utterance [the square bracket indicates what is meant or intended but not said]:

It's a bird. (**Premise**)

[Most birds fly] (*Suppressed psychological premise*)

So, it [probably] flies. (**Conclusion**)

When children say what they are thinking, they rarely say *all* of what they are thinking or talk about what lies behind their thinking; sometimes you'll get nothing more than a 'Yes' or a 'No'. In these cases, teachers/facilitators are presented with no more than the tip of an iceberg. To preserve their autonomy and ownership, uncovering what is below the surface is more like *excavation* than *re-construction*; so, uncover what *they* think (in so far as they're able to say what they think) rather than guess, suggest or surmise what they might mean. From the point of view of the facilitator, it is unclear exactly what the participant means from this utterance (see above). The recommendation, then, in order to maintain an OQM, is to *question further* to *elicit* what they mean. For example (a Non-Dialectically Focused question – see page 47 of Vol. 2):

A: It's a bird, so it flies.

FAC: Could you say a bit more about that? [Opening-up for elicitation – see pages 44–45 of Vol. 2]

Alternatively, here is a more Dialectically Focused approach:

A: It's a bird so it flies.

FAC: Can you say whether you think that means that: *all* birds fly, *most* birds fly, *some* birds fly, or something else? [This approach may require some opening-up – see pages 41–52 and 100–101 of Vol. 2]

This difficulty, of interpreting on behalf of the participants, especially with children, results in, possibly the most difficult aspect of facilitating PhiE: *eliminating paraphrase-responses* (see page 31 of Vol. 2).

Two Aims of PhiE: Dialectic and Inclusion

Part of having an open mindset is that one must work towards meeting an *inclusion aim*. This does not necessarily mean making sure everyone speaks during every session. Actually, by insisting on everyone speaking, it can have the opposite effect, as they exclude themselves having had their 'space invaded'. Meeting the inclusion aim is making everyone feel that they are part of the group, that they can contribute *if they want to*, and then doing your best to make them want to.

It is true that in any given moment, trying to meet the *inclusion aim* (going to those who have not spoken) can mean compromising the other important aim of PhiE: the *dialectical aim* (going deeper with back-and-forth, question-and-answer dialogues between participants). And vice versa: going deeper with the dialectical exchanges can mean compromising the inclusion aim, as it lets some people have more than one go in succession. A good PhiE facilitator tries to keep an eye on both of these aims, attempting to achieve a good balance between them, just as they should between their *presence* and *absence* (see pages 67 of Vol. 1 and 43 of Vol. 2) and the *exploratory* and *justificatory* aims (see page 32).

One should not think of these two aims as necessarily at odds with one another. Having an eye on the inclusion aim – making sure people feel that they can join in, that they are given clear opportunities to do so, and that the facilitator supports their needs so that they go on to contribute – can result in beneficial outcomes for the dialectic. I can't count the number of times reticent members have made important contributions, offering some kind of insight that has taken the discussion to another level, as a result of the facilitator using an inclusionary move or strategy (see page 65 of Vol. 2). If it were left to their volunteering or raising their hand, they would never be heard.

SOCRATIC IRONY AND QUESTIONING MINDSETS

Can one of the central concepts behind PhiE, that of *OQM* (see page 71), really be traced to Socratic origins? Many would say that there is a tension in Socrates: while it is true that he is a master of questioning, in some degree he demonstrates a model example of a *CQM* (see pages xxxiii–xxxiv and 69 of Vol. 1 and 49 and 57–58 of Vol. 2) in that he has hidden agendas behind his questions, i.e., he does not question to know, but to teach the arrogant that they don't really know what they think they know.

Walter Kohan[1] (2008) has suggested that Socrates' general aim is to bring all his interlocutors (and by implication the readers of the dialogues) to realise their ignorance. This means that all those who respond to Socrates' questions can only come to know what Socrates already knows: that they do not know what they think they know. His is a kind of *sceptical imperialism*.

This last point is related to what is known as *Socratic irony*. To many, Socratic irony is the irony the reader apprehends when she witnesses Socrates asking Athenian citizens what something is (e.g., 'What is X?' where 'X' might be 'piety', 'justice', 'beauty', 'love'), where they respond confidently, but where the reader knows full well that they do not really know what they think they know. For example, 'So, tell me now, by Zeus, what you just now maintained you clearly knew: what kind of thing do you say that godliness and ungodliness are . . .?' (*Euthyphro* 5c).

According to this reading of Socratic irony, 'you clearly know' is meant ironically: Socrates *clearly knows* that Euthyphro does not 'clearly know'. An interesting question to ask is: does Socrates, as this reading suggests, share in this irony? Does he already know that they do not know what they think they know? Or does he merely suspect?

There are two ways we might understand Socratic irony (Worley 2011). One is disingenuous, where Socrates is *only pretending* to be ignorant and *only pretending* to value his interlocutor as a source of knowledge. This kind of Socratic irony leads one to see Socrates as a trickster, using rhetorical devices to 'trip up' his arrogant adversaries. It may be argued that something like this is occurring when Socrates is engaged in a more adversarial exchange with, for example, Thrasymachus in the *Republic* or Callicles in the *Gorgias*. However, even in these more pugilistic meetings, Socrates is still interested in a true outcome, more than a victorious one (see pages 42–44). And, this is supported by it being unclear that he 'wins' in either of these exchanges.

The other kind of Socratic irony lies in his *merely suspecting* that his interlocutors do not know what they think they know given that the only thing Socrates is sure of is that *knowing is much more difficult than one might suppose*. When he expresses his own dismay at the end of the *Euthyphro* dialogue, it may be genuine: he may have been hoping that Euthyphro would be able to confer to him something substantive to go to his trial with to be able to persuade the jury of his piety and that his trouble is caused by his own ignorance (16a). It is difficult to ascribe intentions to Socrates, but it is at least not the case that it is a foregone conclusion that his position is ironic.

In the classroom, this reading recommends teachers and facilitators adopt a *tentative voice* (not speaking in absolutes but leaving room for doubt) and a *position of defeasibility* (using language that suggests an acceptance of the possibility of error – see 'Classroom culture' on page 59). This is done so on the basis of an openness to *genuine doubt*. Crucially, this is not disingenuous but it is more tentative; this says, not that (the position of the sceptical imperialist) *we are all (truly) ignorant*, but merely that *we must be open to the real possibility that we don't know what we think we know*.

Socrates is often said to have said, 'The only thing I know is that I know nothing,' which sounds much more like something the sceptical imperialist would say, but this is a much stronger misquote of something he actually says, much more tentatively, in the *Apology*: 'I do not think I know what I do not know' (21d). It follows that one thing he does not know, particularly at the start of an enquiry with an interlocutor is whether the interlocutor will provide him with wisdom. And if it is reasonable to assume that he does not know this, given what he says at 21d, neither does he *think* he knows it.

I would argue, therefore, that Socrates does inhabit an OQM, albeit not all of the time and not unproblematically. His stated ideal, 'the midwifery principle' (see page 69) is consistent with an OQM (and – more than that – seems to demand something like an OQM), his practice, however, is not – at least, not always.

Where we see him in a collaborative mode of engagement, such as when he is enquiring with like-minded friends, then we see him more disposed towards a genuinely open mindset. On one occasion, when in conversation with Glaucon and Adiemantus in the *Republic III*, he explicitly describes what might be entailed by an OQM: '. . . for I myself really don't know yet, but whatever direction the wind of the argument blows us, that's where we must go' (*Republic* 394d).

This seems to go against what Kohan has assumed is a general Socratic epistemological agenda: *to always know that he and his interlocutors are moving away from false belief and towards ignorance*. Socrates is quite explicit here about not knowing where they will end up, and, as any reader of the *Republic* will know, they end up somewhere far from general scepticism. Many will say that this is because Socrates is only a mouthpiece for Plato in the *Republic*. And in this respect, he is, unbeknownst to himself, a tool for another hidden agenda, that of Plato's own substantive theories put forward in *Republic*. Because of the difficulties of separating out the historical from the Platonic Socrates and of attributing doctrines to Plato, I shall assume a continuity between the 'Socrateses' and I generally refrain from talking about 'Platonic' doctrines as distinct from the Socratic.[2]

With qualifications (see page 42), the correct mindset for PhiE is what can be seen when Socrates is in a more collaborative (*dialectic*) and less combative (*eristic*)[3] mode of conversational exchange. And it is the former that we aim to imitate in PhiE, so, in this respect an OQM is, with qualification, an ideal Socratic mindset (see also page 69 for more on 'ideal Socratic practice').

[1]My thanks to Walter for helpful comments on this section.
[2]See page 20 and footnote 1 on p. 70.
[3]From 'Eris' the god of 'strife'. See Plato's *Euthydemus* for the distinction between eristic/dialectic approaches.

IN SUMMARY

PhiE is, in principle, very simple. It asks a certain kind of question, first used by Heraclitus (see page 14), that is *grammatically closed* and *conceptually open* (see page 14 of Vol. 2) in order to allow a *dialectical* exploration and investigation of the question to unfold (see page 15). The 'question' (see page 13 of Vol. 2) may be in question form or in a *questioning mode*: beginning with some kind of wonder, uneasiness, or uncertainty about an observation, an experience, event or personal act.[9] The group is then engaged *intuitively* and naturally with a particular question type and question formulation by following simple, dialectical progress drawn from Parmenides and a development of his *conditions of dialectic*: namely, the group is invited to respond to the question by *thinking*, *speaking* and *listening* (in no particular order – see page 2 of Vol. 2).

Following some explicit descriptions of ideal practice by Socrates in Plato, the facilitator adopts a particular kind of *mindset*, one that emphasises a minimal *presence* (which focuses on the structural aspect of the discussion, impartially) and an unusual personal *absence* (see page 67), centralising participant/group-centred *critical listening* (see page 27 of Vol. 2) that attempts to elicit and uncover the participants' intended, unique meanings rather than focusing on surface meaning and logical implications and entailments of utterances (see page 74).

The use of *OQM* and *absence* (see page 67) optimises the groups' *autonomy* (see page 34), *ownership* (see page 66), and sense of place, or *topography* (to make reference to a word often used by Aristotle in discussions about dialectical enquiry: *topos*[10]) in an enquiry.

The facilitator also deepens the critical aspect of the discussions by using specific dialectical questioning techniques and strategies that have a precedent in Plato. Chiefly (though not only) these are pursuing *hypothesis thinking* ('If . . . then . . .') and *justification* ('I think . . . because . . .'). This is achieved through the *if-ing*, *anchoring* and *opening-up* strategies (see page Part Two of Vol. 2).

If the facilitator asks the right kind of question, then invites the participants to respond to it and allows the *dialectical triangle* of thinking, speaking and listening to take its course, and, as long as the facilitator adopts an OQM (see page 71) and listens well, not only should a philosophical enquiry occur but it should also progress well, with no more than a little attendance to the structure by the facilitator where necessary. This is so simple that it can be done with nursery children as well as PhD students. As we see in the slave boy in Plato's *Meno* (see link provided in footnote 4 on page 71), the capacity to philosophise is within most of us and all that is needed is the right conditions for this capacity to be activated. PhiE provides those conditions.

To see how these principles have been realised into classroom practice for modern schools and other settings, now turn to *Corrupting Youth*, Volume 2.

NOTES

1. Berys and Morag Gaut have also developed a closed-question approach to doing philosophy with the very young. See their books *Philosophy for Young Children* and *Philosophy for Older Children* (Routledge). See also the work of Sara Stanley (2012) and Erik Kenyon (2019) with the very young.

2. Often quoted as 'philosophy begins in wonder'. Aristotle also said something similar in *Metaphysics* (982b): 'For it is owing to their wonder that men both now begin and at first began to philosophise'.

3. Literally, 'without which not'.

4. It's worth sharing that this insight came to me when TPF specialist invited actor/improvisor Oliver Senton to run an improvisation workshop for us. He kept saying, 'I know, as philosophers, that you're supposed to think, but try not to think, just let things happen!' This provocation got me thinking about how these two ways of thinking might be reconciled in our work.

5. Thanks to TPF specialist Steven Campbell Harris for this expression.

6. Compare this list to the basic dialectical model drawn from McCabe's analysis of Heraclitus on page 17. This one is a development of that one.

7. See Thinking Moves: metacognition made simple (footnote 5 on page 114 of Vol. 2) for more on 'thinking ahead' and 'thinking back'.

8. This section summarises the paper Ariadne's Clew (Worley 2016).

9. Thanks to Pieter Mostert for this list of what I have characterised as a 'questioning mode' – see also Dillon's distinction between *asking a question* and *putting something into question* (see page 67 of Vol. 2).

10. This is where our word 'topic' comes from. And, tellingly, 'Topics' is the title of Aristotle's major work on dialectic.

Appendix 1

Dialogue-Based Practice and Research and Links to PhiE

This section draws from relevant research from a very helpful overview of research that supports dialogic learning by Alina Reznitzkaya in her recent paper *The Emperor with No Clothes* (2020). I have also drawn correspondence between the research and PhiE by directing the reader to the relevant section in this book and its sister volume. I should point out that none of this research has been done with PhiE directly but much of it corresponds with or is consistent with PhiE's pedagogical principles. I have noted where qualifications are needed or where PhiE diverges from other practices.

Here are the dialogical-pedagogical approaches around which much of the following research and recommendations have been based: *Philosophy for Children* (Faira et al. 2015; Lipman 2003; Sharp 1991), *Collaborative Reasoning* (Lin et al. 2012; Waggoner et al. 1995), *Argue with Me* (Kuhn et al. 2016), *Thinking Together* (Dawes et al. 2004), and *Accountable Talk* (Michaels et al. 2002).

The research includes the following: Alexander 2006; Applebee et al. 2003; Billings and Fitzgerald 2002; Chinn et al. 2001; Murphy et al. 2009; Nystrand et al. 2003; Resnick et al. 2015; Reznitskaya and Gregory 2013; Kim et al. 2019. Any principles or recommendations drawn from these practices and this body of research and summarised by Reznitskaya has been highlighted below in **bold**.

COGNITION

PhiE requires that students engage in **cognitive elaboration**; as a basic requirement it asks participants to **explain** themselves and to **justify** their claims (see 'The basic mechanism of PhiE' on page 3 of Vol. 2 and the

Platonic dialectical principles of *hypothesis* and *justification* on page 20 in Vol. 1). In addition to this it also requires that both participants (and the facilitator to some extent) be in a flexible and dynamic mindset (see 'Open Questioning Mindset' on page 71 of Vol. 1), ready to **reorganise their mental models** (see 'The 4 'R's' on page 4 of Vol. 1), to **uncover and correct gaps** (Chi 2000; N. Webb 2009 – see pages 29, 9–11, 63 of Vol. 1).

CONSTRUCTIVIST

In line with **cognitive-constructivist** theories of Piaget (e.g., 1932), PhiE also promotes **cognitive conflict** (when new knowledge contradicts already held knowledge) and **cognitive dissonance** (where a set of one's beliefs or attitudes are at odds with another set – see pages 60 of Vol. 1 and 11–12, 35 and 38 of Vol. 2). It also provides the time, and the setting to be able to **consider** (see 'Listening as 'considering'' on pages 27–33 of Vol. 2) these conflicts and dissonances and to set out towards **solutions** and resolutions through **exploratory talk** (Mercer 2003; Wegerif et al. 1999). This is done critically yet constructively by **considered engagement with one another's ideas, claims, statements and suggestions** (P. Webb and Treagust 2006).

ORDINARY LANGUAGE

PhiE is both Socratic and Vygotskian in that it proceeds with doing philosophy through (mainly *ordinary*) **language as the primary mode of engagement** and by **critical co-construction of knowledge, attitudes and beliefs of the group members** (Vygotsky 1968, 1981). See pages xxx and 36 of Vol. 1.

INTERNALISATION

PhiE is also Aristotelian, as well as Vygotskian, in that it promotes **habituation and internalisation** (see page 31 of Vol. 1 and 'Silent dialogue' on page 72 of Vol. 2) by repeatedly engaging in philosophical enquiries and repeating thinking opportunities with accompanying **cognitive prompts** from the facilitator (e.g., certain kinds of questioning) designed to make the appropriate **cultural tools** (e.g., **providing reasons, questioning someone critically, asking for clarification or justification) available to the group** (Reznitskaya and Gregory 2013; N. Webb 2009; Wilkinson et al. 2015). See 'Part Two: Expert facilitation, managing dialectic' on page 41 of Vol. 2.

SCAFFOLDING

PhiE is particularly well-developed when it comes to the **scaffolding** principles and approaches of the facilitator (Brownfield and Wilkinson 2018; van de Pol et al. 2010). A PhiE facilitator does not merely listen and ask for participants to say what they think or to respond to one another, they have sophisticated tools and methods for eliciting **arguments** from the participants (e.g., 'Anchoring and opening-up' on pages 41–54 of Vol. 2), of having them **develop their arguments** (e.g., 'If-ing, anchoring and opening-up' on pages 41–62 and also page 81 of Vol. 2 and onwards), or **build on them** (e.g., 'Double anchor' on page 67 of Vol. 2), or by bringing the group to consider conceptual variables (e.g., 'Either-or-the-if' on page 58 of Vol. 2) and so on.

PhiE fits well with the following **four aspects of scaffolding** practice:

PhiE is **supportive**, gentle and caring, and **contingent**, or sensitive to particular pupil's needs (see Vol. 1: 'Friendship' on page 37, 'Interest and Engagement' on page 55, 'The Need for Conditions' on page 56, 'The Conditions' on page 57, 'Classroom Culture' on page 59, 'PhiE Begins with Intuitions' on page 60 and 'Two Aims of PhiE: Dialectic and Inclusion' on page 76; Vol. 2: see 'Listen: Listening' on page 27, 'Paraphrasing' on page 31, 'Other Key Dispositions in PhiE' on page 34, 'Inclusionary Moves' on page 65 and 'The Emergent Question Approach' on page 66).

PhiE is also **fading** in that it has numerous ways, including **coaching** methods, of **transferring responsibility** of the philosophical and dialectical skills to the participants over time (see Vol. 2: 'The Imaginary Disagreer: Silent Dialogue in the classroom' on page 74, 'The Mapper and PIES(S) Questions' on page 83 and the whole of Part 3: Advanced Facilitation: taking things further on pages 87–115, especially 'Writing in PhiE' on page 88, 'Self-facilitation' on page 92 and 'Metacognition and extended thinking in PhiE' on page 94).

PhiE has a multitude of **talk moves** (O'Connor et al. 2015, p. 112) that through facilitator **modelling** and **fading techniques** (see above) the facilitator encourages participants to **make their own contributions** (see fading methods in PhiE above), to **listen to each other** (see 'Listen: Listening' on page 27), to **keep the focus on reasoning** (see, especially, 'Part Two: Expert facilitation, managing dialectic') and to **work respectfully and productively with the ideas of others**: the entire method of PhiE aims to achieve this latter aspect. (See also tables 1, 2, 3 and 4 on pages 131–145 in Vol. 2 for an extensive list of the key facilitator/talk moves, many of which are eventually transferred to the group when PhiE is run with a group for sufficient time.)

PhiE can be understood as **constructivist** for a number of reasons: the role of the participants in a PhiE is **active**, not passive; the principle emphasis is on their **verbal activities** (see 'The dialectical triangle' on page 2 of Vol. 2), though reading and writing may have a role in a PhiE (see 'Writing in PhiE' on page 88 of Vol. 2 and 'Session plan 4: Metaphysics through text' on page 125 of Vol. 2); the participants are required to verbally **articulate**, **explain** and **justify** their ideas to others (see 'Truth and Knowledge' on page 63 of Vol. 1 and 'The basic mechanism of PhiE' on page 3 of Vol. 2).

THE FACILITATOR

A facilitator in PhiE **models** philosophical method, **coaches** the self-facilitation of the group, **teaches** curriculum content, thinking moves and critical thinking skills, acts as a **conceptual change agent**, they **mentor apprentices**, and **support a community of learners** (Windschitl 2002, p. 135) (see page 26 of Vol. 1 and pages 92 and 94 of Vol. 2).

According to the research, teachers facilitating dialogic, enquiry-based learning, tend to **ask for clarification** (seeing 'Opening-up' on pages 41–51 esp. 44 of Vol. 2), **prompt for alternative perspectives** (see 'Silent-Dialogue' on page 72 in Vol. 2, 'The Imaginary Disagreer: Silent Dialogue in the classroom' on page 74 in Vol. 2) and encourage **connection-making and relating** (see 'Connects' on page 53 and 'Connect things up with dialectical questioning' on page 89 of Vol. 2, 'Thinking tools and thinking wall' on page 98).

PARTICIPANTS

And during PhiE, students often **'take up' each other's line of inquiry**. This is at the heart of any dialectical practice as I have defined it (see pages 17, 26 and 62 of Vol. 1) and therefore it is at the heart of PhiE. Student responses should also be **'chained onto coherent lines of inquiry'** (Alexander 2003), they should **listen to and react to each other's positions and justifications** and these elements can be found in the PhiE practices of *Right to reply* (see page 63 of Vol. 2), *Response Detector* moves (see 'The Response Detector and the third way' on page 62 of Vol. 2) and that of *holding someone to account* (see 'Right to Reply' on pages 63–64 'Classroom Culture' on page 59 of Vol. 1. See also 'Listen: Listening' on page 27 of Vol. 2).

SOCIAL PRACTICES

The social practices in PhiE **support the learning of higher-order competencies** such as **critical thinking skills** and **argumentation** by adopting a more **egalitarian social organisation**, and **conferring more authority to the group over the content and form of the discourse.** Although PhiE recognises that each individual within the group has an *equal right* to speak (see page 44 in Vol. 1) and to have their ideas given *equally fair consideration* (see 'Listening as considering' on page 28 of Vol. 2), it does not assume that all contributions are of equal philosophical *value*; some ideas are more useful, more insightful, more nuanced, valid or sound, critically successful and so on (see page 41 in Vol. 1, 'Excellence and competition' on page 42). So, although PhiE is *egalitarian*, it does not subordinate the quality of rational, philosophical discourse to egalitarianism. The same can be said for the **authority over the content, self-selected turn-taking,** the **asking of questions,** the **introduction of new topics and the suggestion of procedural changes.** The participants **determine the direction of the conversation** in PhiE with the caveat that there will be instances where the curriculum or other pedagogical priorities take precedence over the participants' autonomy, interests and direction (see 'Philosophical process and content' on page 1 of Vol. 2 and 'Anchoring and remits' on page 70 of Vol. 2, 'The Sibelius Model' on page 87 of Vol. 2 and 'Session plan 2: Ethics through a question' on page 118 in Vol. 2).

PROBLEMATISING

PhiE is **problematising** in that it always seeks divergence, controversy and promotes dissent whilst, at the same time, promoting **collaboration towards resolving problems** (see 'Logos and Flux' on page 4 of Vol. 1): PhiE is the synthesis of opposition and collaboration par excellence (see 'Dissent' on page 33 of Vol. 1). It pursues **open-ended questions**, although, practically speaking, PhiE makes use of a guided, closed questioning technique to do so (see 'Think and Speak: Questions in PhiE' on page 13 of Vol. 2).

PhiE minimises procedures (e.g., gathering questions and voting) in order to give more of any allotted time to enquiry (see 'Think: The stimulus' on page 10 of Vol. 2). This allows participants to be able to **give more elaborate contributions,** to give an issue, question or topic **lengthy and revised consideration and re-consideration,** to more fully **explain their ideas to others** so that they may be better understood (e.g., Alexander, 2005; Beck et al. 1996; Chinn et al. 2001; Reznitskaya et al. 2012).

As with other dialogical pedagogies, PhiE **contrasts with 'sage on the stage' transmission models,** where students are **rewarded or punished in order that certain beliefs and knowledge are shaped in them.** PhiE **eschews the traditional 'IRE'** (or *Initiate, Response, Evaluate*) **exchange patterns** between students and teacher, certainly with regard to the last, where PhiE puts the onus of evaluation back to the group (e.g., Alexander 2008; Alvermann et al. 1990; Henning and Lockhart 2003; Howe and Abedin 2013; Mehan 1998; Nystrand et al. 2003; Onosko 1990).

APPENDIX 1 REFERENCES AND BIBLIOGRAPHY

Alexander, R. J. (2003). *Talk for Learning: The First Year*. Northallerton: North Yorkshire County Council.

Alexander, R. J. (2005, July). *Culture, Dialogue and Learning: Notes on an Emerging Pedagogy*. Paper presented at the Conference of the International Association for Cognitive Education and Psychology, University of Durham, UK.

Alexander, R. J. (2006). *Towards Dialogic Teaching: Rethinking Classroom Talk* (3rd ed.). York, UK: Dialogos.

Alexander, R. J. (2008). *Essays on Pedagogy*. New York: Routledge.

Alvermann, D. E., O'Brien, D. G. and Dillon, D. R. (1990). What teachers do when they say they're having discussions of content area reading assignments: A qualitative analysis. *Reading Research Quarterly, 25*, 296–322.

Applebee, A. N., Langer, J. A., Nystrand, M. and Gamoran, A. (2003). Discussion-based approaches to developing understanding: Classroom instruction and student performance in middle and high school English. *American Educational Research Journal, 40*(3), 685–730. doi:10.3102/00028312040003685

Beck, I. L., McKeown, M. G., Sandora, C., Kucan, L. and Worthy, J. (1996). Questioning the author: A year-long classroom implementation to engage students with text. *The Elementary School Journal, 96*(4), 385–414.

Billings, L. and Fitzgerald, J. (2002). Dialogic discussion and the Paideia seminar. *American Educational Research Journal, 39*(4), 907–941. doi:10.3102/00028312039004905

Brownfield, K. and Wilkinson, I. A. G. (2018). Examining the impact of scaffolding on literacy learning: A critical examination of research and guidelines to advance inquiry. *International Journal of Educational Research, 90*, 177–190. doi:10.1016/j.ijer.2018.01.004

Chi, M. T. H. (2000). Self-explaining expository texts: The dual processes of generating inferences and repairing mental models. In R. Glaser (Ed.), *Advances in Instructional Psychology: Educational Design and Cognitive Science* (pp. 161–238). Hillsdale, NJ: Erlbaum.

Chinn, C. A., Anderson, R. C. and Waggoner, M. A. (2001). Patterns of discourse in two kinds of literature discussion. *Reading Research Quarterly, 36*(4), 378–411. doi:10.1598/RRQ.36.4.3

Dawes, L., Mercer, N. and Wegerif, R. (2004). *Thinking Together: A Programme of Activities for Developing Speaking, Listening and Thinking Skills for Children Aged 8–11*. Birmingham, UK: Imaginative Minds.

Faira, F., Haasa, L. E., Gardosikb, C., Johnsona, D., Pricea, D. and Leipnika, O. (2015). Socrates in the schools: Gains at three-year follow-up. *Journal of Philosophy in Schools, 2*(2).

Henning, J. and Lockhart, A. (2003). Acquiring art of classroom discourse: A comparison of teacher and preservice teacher talk in a fifth grade classroom. *Research for Educational Reform, 8*(3), 46–57.

Howe, C. and Abedin, M. (2013). Classroom dialogue: A systematic review across four decades of research. *Cambridge Journal of Education, 43*(3), 325–356. doi:1 0.1080/0305764X.2013.786024

Kim, M.-Y. and Wilkinson, I. A. G. (2019). What is dialogic teaching? Constructing, deconstructing, and reconstructing a pedagogy of classroom talk. *Learning, Culture and Social Interaction, 21*, 70–86. doi: 10.1016/j.lcsi.2019.02.003

Kuhn, D., Hemberger, L. and Khait, V. (2016). *Argue with me: Argument as a path to developing students' thinking and writing.* New York: Routledge.

Lin, T.-J., Anderson, R. C., Jadallah, M., Kuo, L., Wu, X., Hummel, J. E., … Dong, T. (2012). Children's use of analogy during Collaborative Reasoning. *Child development, 83*(4), 1429–1443.

Lipman, M. (2003). *Thinking in Education.* New York, NY: Cambridge University Press.

Mehan, H. (1998). The study of social interaction in educational settings: Accomplishments and unresolved issues. *Human Development, 41*(4), 245–269. doi:10.1159/000022586

Mercer, N. (2003). Development through dialogue. In T. Grainger (Ed.), *The Routledge Falmer Reader in Language and Literacy* (pp. 121–137). New York: Routledge.

Mercer, N., Wegerif, R. and Major, L. (Eds.). (2019). *The Routledge International Handbook of Research on Dialogic Education.* Abingdon, UK: Routledge.

Michaels, S., O'Connor, M. C., Hall, M. W. and Resnick, L. B. (2002). *Accountable Talk: Classroom Conversation That Works (3 CD-ROM Set).* Pittsburgh, PA: University of Pittsburgh.

Murphy, P. K., Wilkinson, I. A. G., Soter, A., Hennessey, M. N. and Alexander, J. F. (2009). Examining the effects of classroom discussion on students' comprehension of text: A meta-analysis. *Journal of Educational Psychology, 101*(3), 740–764. doi:10.1037/a0015576

Nystrand, M., Wu, L., Gamoran, A., Zeiser, S. and Long, D. A. (2003). Questions in time: Investigating the structure and dynamics of unfolding classroom discourse. *Discourse Processes, 35*(2), 135–198.

O'Connor, C., Michaels, S. and Chapin, S. (2015). Scaling down to explore the role of talk in learning: From district intervention to controlled classroom study. In L. B. Resnick, C. Asterhan and S. N. Clarke (Eds.), *Socializing Intelligence through Talk and Dialogue.* Washington, DC: American Educational Research Association.

Onosko, J. J. (1990). Comparing teacher instruction to promote students' thinking. *Journal of Curriculum Studies, 22*(5), 443–461.

Piaget, J. (1932). *The Moral Judgment of the Child.* London: Routledge & Kegan Paul.

Resnick, L. B., Asterhan, C. S. C. and Clarke, S. N. (2015). *Socializing Intelligence Through Academic Talk and Dialogue.* Washington, DC: American Educational Research Association.

Reznitskaya, A., Glina, M., Carolan, B., Michaud, O., Rogers, J. and Sequeira, L. (2012). Examining transfer effects from dialogic discussions to new tasks and contexts. *Contemporary Educational Psychology, 37*, 288–306. doi:10.1016/j.cedpsych.2012.02.003

Reznitskaya, A. (2020). *The Emperor with No Clothes* (unpublished at time of writing).

Reznitskaya, A. and Gregory, M. (2013). Student thought and classroom language: Examining the mechanisms of change in dialogic teaching. *Educational Psychologist, 48*(2), 114–133.

Sharp, A. M. (1991). The community of inquiry: Education for democracy. *Thinking: The Journal of Philosophy for Children, 9*(2), 31–37.

van de Pol, J., Volman, M. and Beishuizen, J. (2010). Scaffolding in teacher–student interaction: A decade of research. *Educational Psychology Review, 22*(3), 271–296. doi:10.1007/s10648-010-9127-6

Vygotsky, L. S. (1968). *Thought and Language* (Newly Revised, Translated, and Edited by Alex Kozulin). Cambridge, MA: MIT Press.

Vygotsky, L. S. (1981). The genesis of higher-order mental functions. In J. V. Wertsch (Ed.), *The Concept of Activity in Soviet Psychology* (pp. 144–188). Armonk, NY: Sharpe.

Waggoner, M., Chinn, C. A., Yi, H. and Anderson, R. C. (1995). Collaborative reasoning about stories. *Language Arts, 72*, 582–589.

Webb, N. (2009). The teacher's role in promoting collaborative dialogue in the classroom. *British Journal of Educational Psychology, 79*(1), 1–28.

Webb, P. and Treagust, D. F. (2006). Using exploratory talk to enhance problem-solving and reasoning skills in grade-7 science classrooms. *Research in Science Education, 36*(4), 381–401. doi:10.1007/s11165-005-9011-4

Wegerif, R., Mercer, N. and Dawes, L. (1999). From social interaction to individual reasoning: An empirical investigation of a possible sociocultural model of cognitive development. *Learning and Instruction, 9*(6), 493–516. doi:10.1016/S0959-4752(99)00013-4

Wilkinson, I. A. G., Murphy, P. K. and Binici, S. (2015). Dialogue-intensive pedagogies for promoting reading comprehension: What we know, what we need to know. In L. B. Resnick, C. A. Asterhan and S. N. Clarke (Eds.), *Socializing Intelligence Through Academic Talk and Dialogue* (pp. 37–50). Washington, DC: American Educational Research Association.

Windschitl, M. (2002). Framing constructivism in practice as the negotiation of dilemmas: An analysis of the conceptual, pedagogical, cultural, and political challenges facing teachers. *Review of Educational Research, 72*(2), 131–175. doi:10.3102/00346543072002131

Bibliography (Volume 1)

Arendt, H. *The Life of the Mind*. Volume 1: *Thinking* and Volume 2: *Willing*. San Diego: Harcourt Press, 1977/1978.

Aristophanes. *Lysistrata and Other Plays*. Translated by Alan H. Sommerstein. Revised Ed edition. London; New York: Penguin Classics, 2003.

Baggini, J. *How the World Thinks: A Global History of Philosophy*. Granta, 2018.

Barnes, J. *Early Greek Philosophy*. Harmondsworth, Middlesex; New York: Penguin, 1987.

Benson, H. *Blackwell Companions to Philosophy: A Companion to Plato*. Wiley-Blackwell, 2009.

Bowker, M. H. 'Teaching students to ask questions instead of answering them', *Thought and Action* 26, no. 1 (2017), 127–134.

Bowyer, L., Amos, C., and Stevens, D. 'What is "philosophy"? Understandings of philosophy circulating in the literature on the teaching and learning of philosophy in schools', *Journal of Philosophy in Schools* 7, no. 1 (2020), 38–67. doi:10.46707/jps.v7i.108.

Cassidy, C., Christie, D., Marwick, H., Deeney, L., McLean, G., and Rogers, K. 'Fostering citizenship in marginalised children through participation in community of philosophical inquiry', *Education, Citizenship and Social Justice* 13, no. 2 (2018), 120–132. doi:10.1177/1746197917700151.

Colom, R., García Moriyón, F., Magro, C., and Morilla, E. 'The long-term impact of philosophy for children: A longitudinal study (preliminary results)', *Analytic Teaching and Philosophical Praxis* 35, no. 1 (2014).

Cooper, J. M. *Plato: Complete Works*. Indianapolis, IN: Hackett Publishing, 1997.

D'Angour, Armand. *Socrates in Love: The Making of a Philosopher*. London: Bloomsbury, 2019.

Eastop, Eastop and Hartley's 'difference exchange': http://www.differenceexchange.com/about.htm

Facione, Peter (ed.). 'Report on critical thinking', American Philosophical Association Subcommittee on Pre-College Philosophy, University of Delaware, 1989.

Fisher, R. *Games for Thinking.* Nash Pollock Publishing, 1997a.

Fisher, R. *Poems for Thinking.* Nash Pollock Publishing, 1997b.

Fisher, R. *Stories for Thinking.* Nash Pollock Publishing, 1997c.

Fisher, R. *Values for Thinking.* Nash Pollock Publishing, 2001.

Frunza, Mihaela. "'Philosophy in action" in the texts and practices of Peter Worley', *Studia Universitatis Babeş-Bolyai Philosophia* 64, no. 3 (2019), 25–40.

Gaut, Berys and Gaut Morag. *Philosophy for Young Children: A Practical Guide.* London; New York: Taylor and Francis, 2011.

Gregory, M. R., Joanna Haynes, and Karin Murris. *The Routledge International Handbook of Philosophy for Children.* 1st Edition (Hardback). New York: Routledge, 2016.

Goldstein, quoted in Arnold H. Modell. *The Private Self.* Cambridge, MA: Harvard University Press, 1993, p. 44.

Gopnik, Alison. *The Philosophical Baby: What Children's Minds Tell Us About Truth, Love, and the Meaning of Life.* New York: Picador, 2009.

Gopnik, A., Kuhl, P., and Meltzoff, A. *The Scientist in the Crib: What Early Learning Tells Us About the Mind.* New York: Perennial Books, 1999.

Gorard, Stephen, Nadia Siddiqui, and Beng Huat See. Philosophy for children: Evaluation report and executive summary. Education Endowment Foundation, 2015. https://educationendowmentfoundation.org.uk/public/files/Projects/Eval uation_Reports/EEF_Project_Report_PhilosophyForChildren.pdf

Gygax, E. Gary, Dave Arneson (revised by Frank Mentzer) *Dungeons and Dragons.* TSR Hobbies 1974, 1977, 1978, 1981, 1983.

Habermas, Jurgen. 'Discourse Ethics: Notes on a Program of Philosophical Justification', *Moral Consciousness and Communicative Action,* trans. Christian Lenhart and Shierry Weber Nicholson. Cambridge: MIT Press, 1990, pp. 43–115.

Hadot, Pierre. *What Is Ancient Philosophy?* Cambridge, MA: Harvard University Press, 2002.

Hall, Edith. *The Ancient Greeks: Ten Ways They Shaped the Modern World.* Vintage, 2015.

Haynes, Joanna and Murris, Karin. *Picturebooks, Pedagogy and Philosophy.* London: Routledge Research in Education, 2011.

Herodotus. *The Histories.* Translated by G. Rawlinson and Edited by H. Bowden. Everyman, 1992.

Higgins, Charlotte. *It's All Greek to Me.* London: Short Books, 2008.

Hughes, B. *The Hemlock Cup: Socrates, Athens and the Search for the Good Life.* First Paperback Edition. London: Vintage, 2011.

Jackson, Steve and Ian Livingstone. *Fighting Fantasy Gamebooks Series.* Puffin, 1982.

Joyce, James. *Ulysses.* First published in Paris in 1922 (2010).

Kahneman, D. *Thinking, Fast and Slow.* New York: Penguin, 2012.

Kenyon, Erik. *Ethics for the Very Young.* Lanham, MD: Rowman & Littlefield, 2019.

Kohan Walter Oman. Sócrates: la paradoja de enseñar y aprender. *dans* Livio Rossetti-Alessandro Stavru (eds.), *Socratica 2008. Studies dans Ancient Socratic Literature,* Bari, Levante editori *Le Rane—Collana di Studi e Testi,* 2010, 159–184.

Kuhn, D., and D. A. Dean 'Bridge between cognitive psychology and educational practice', *Theory into Practice* 43, no. 4 (2004), 268–273.

Law, Stephen. *The Philosophy Files*. Orion Children's Books, 2011.

Leigh, Fiona. 'Platonic dialogue, maieutic method and critical thinking', *Journal of Philosophy of Education* 41, no. 3 (2007), 309–323.

Leroi, Armand Marie. *The Lagoon: How Aristotle Invented Science*. Translation edition. New York: Viking Books, 2014.

Locke, John. *Some Thoughts Concerning Education and Of the Conduct of the Understanding*. Indianapolis, IN: Hackett, 1996.

Mackenzie (now McCabe), Mary Margaret. 'Heraclitus and the art of paradox', *Oxford Studies in Ancient Philosophy*, 1988 (reprinted in Platonic Conversations, 2015).

Mackenzie (now McCabe), Mary Margaret. *Parmenides' Dilemma in Phronesis*, 1982 (reprinted in Platonic Conversations, 2015—see below).

Maslow, A. H. 'A theory of human motivation', *Psychological Review* 50 (1943), 370–396.

Matthews, Gareth. *Philosophy and the Young Child*. Cambridge, MA: Harvard University Press, 1980.

McCabe, Mary, Margaret. 'Chapter 1: Platonic Conversations', in *Platonic Conversations*. Oxford University Press, 2015.

McCabe, Mary, Margaret. 'Is dialectic as dialectic does? The virtue of philosophical conversation', *The Virtuous Life in Greek Ethics*, ed. B. Reis, Cambridge University Press, 2006 (reprinted in *Platonic Conversations*, 2015).

McCabe, Mary, Margaret. *Platonic Conversations*. Oxford University Press, 2015.

McCall, Catherine. *Transforming Thinking: Philosophical Inquiry in the Primary and Secondary Classroom*. Routledge, 2009.

McGinn, Colin. *Shakespeare's Philosophy*. Harper Collins, 2006.

Michel de Montaigne. *The Complete Essays*. Editor and translator M. A. Screech. Penguin, 1991.

Miller, James (ed.) *Lives of the Eminent Philosophers* by Diogenes Laertius. Translated by Pamela Mensch. Oxford University Press, 2018.

Murris, Karin. *Teaching Philosophy with Picture Books* (out of print), 1992b.

Nehamas, Alexander. *The Art of Living: Socratic Reflections from Plato to Foucault*. Berkeley: University of California Press, 1998.

O'Connell, Mark. 'The courage of ambivalence', *BBC Radio 4 programme*. https://www.bbc.co.uk/sounds/play/m0007k73; https://www.theguardian.com/technology/2016/mar/26/microsoft-deeply-sorry-for-offensive-tweets-by-ai-chatbot

O'Connor, Eugene. *The Essential Epicurus*. Prometheus Books, 1993.

Pappas, Nickolas. *Routledge Philosophy GuideBook to Plato and the Republic*. 2nd edition. London; New York: Routledge, 2003.

Perseus (*Apology*, Plato): http://www.perseus.tufts.edu/hopper/text?doc=Perseus%3Atext%3A1999.01.0169%3Atext%3DApol.%3Asection%3D24b

Rawls, John. *A Theory of Justice*. Reissue edition. Cambridge, MA: Harvard University Press, 2005.

Reznitskaya, A., and Ian A. G. Wilkinson. *The Most Reasonable Answer: Helping Students Build Better Arguments Together*. Harvard Education Press, 2017.

Robinson, Richard, 1953. 'Plato's Earlier Dialectic', in Kerferd, G. B. *The Classical Review* 5, no. 1 (1955), 50–52. Accessed February 10, 2020. www.jstor.org/stable/705113.

Rogers, Carl. *On Becoming a Person*, 1961, 350–351.

Rutherford, Adam, *How to Argue with a Racist: History, Science, Race and Reality*. Weidenfeld & Nicolson, 2020.

Scott, Michael. *The Greatest Show on Earth*. Open University. https://www.open.edu /openlearn/tv-radio-events/tv/ancient-greece-the-greatest-show-on-earth

Shapiro, David A. *Plato Was Wrong! Footnotes on Doing Philosophy with Young People*. Lanham, MD: R&L Education, 2012.

Siddiqui, Nadia, Stephen Gorard, and Beng Huat See. Non-cognitive impacts of philosophy for children. Project Report. Durham, NC: School of Education, Durham University, School of Education, 2017. http://dro.dur.ac.uk/20880/1/20880.pdf?D DD34+DDD29+czwc58+d700tmt.

Soanes, C., and Angus Stevenson (eds.). *Oxford Dictionary of English*. 2nd edition. Oxford University Press, 2003, 2005.

Sophocles, and Bernard Knox. *The Three Theban Plays: 'Antigone', 'Oedipus the King', 'Oedipus at Colonus'*. Translated by Robert Fagles. 1st edition. Harmondsworth, Middlesex; New York, NY: Penguin, 1984.

Sousanis, Nick. *Unflattening*. Cambridge, MA: Harvard University Press, 2015.

Sprod, Tim. '(2) Book review—40 lessons to get children thinking: Philosophical thought adventures across the curriculum', Accessed 27 February 2020. https://ww w.researchgate.net/publication/321880957_Book_review_-_40_lessons_to_get_ch ildren_thinking_Philosophical_thought_adventures_across_the_curriculum

Stanley, Sarah. *Why Think?: Philosophical Play from 3–11*. New York: Continuum, 2012.

Sullivan, Wendy and Judy Rees. *Clean Language: Revealing Metaphors and Opening Minds*. Crown House, 2008.

Thucydides. *The Peloponnesian War*. Revised ed. edition. Oxford; New York: OUP Oxford, 2009.

Trickey, Steve. 'Promoting social and cognitive development in schools: An evaluation of "thinking through philosophy"', 2007. http://www.ep.liu.se/ecp/021/vol1 /026/

Trickey, S., and K. J. Topping. "Philosophy for children": A systematic review', *Research Papers in Education* 19, no. 3 (2004), 365–380. doi:10.1080/02671520 42000248016.

Vernon, Mark. 'Philosophy as awakening' parts 1 and 2. https://www.markvernon.co m/philosophy-as-awakening; https://www.markvernon.com/philosophy-as-awak ening-for-the-stoics-epicureans-and-others

Warburton, Nigel. 'Without conversation, philosophy is just dogma—Aeon essays', *Aeon*, 2013. Accessed 4 May 2020. https://aeon.co/essays/without-conversation-p hilosophy-is-just-dogma

Wartenberg, Thomas. *Big Ideas for Little Kids*. 2nd edition. Rowman & Littlefield Education, 2009, 2014.

West, Andy. https://www.theguardian.com/commentisfree/2015/nov/19/philosophy-poverty-drugs-kids-young-people

Wittgenstein, Ludwig. *Philosophical Investigations*. Edited by P. M. S. Hacker and Joachim Schulte. 4th edition. Chichester, West Sussex, U.K.; Malden, MA: Wiley-Blackwell, 2009.

Worley, E., and Worley, P. 'Teaching critical thinking and metacognitive skills through philosophical enquiry: A practitioners report on experiments in the classroom', *Childhood and Philosophy* 15(2019c), 1–34.

Worley, Peter. *100 Ideas for Primary Teachers: Questioning*. Bloomsbury, 2019a.

Worley, Peter. *40 Lessons to Get Children Thinking: Philosophical Thought Adventures across the Curriculum*. Bloomsbury, 2015b.

Worley, Peter. 'Ariadne's clew: Absence and presence in the facilitation of philosophical conversations'. *Journal of Philosophy in Schools*, 3, no. (2 (2016), 51–70).

Worley, Peter. *Once Upon an If: The Storythinking Handbook*. Bloomsbury, 2016.

Worley, Peter. 'Open thinking, closed questioning: Two kinds of open and closed question', in the *Journal of Philosophy in Schools*, 2, no. 2 (2015a), 17–292015a.

Worley, Peter. 'Socratic Irony in the Classroom', for Innovate My School: http://www.innovatemyschool.com/ideas/socratic-irony-in-the-classroom-clouseau-or-columbo

Worley, Peter. TES competition think piece: 'Tomorrow's Teacher: Learning from the past': file:///Users/peterworley/Downloads/Tomorrow's%20Teacher%20-%20learning%20from%20the%20past%20by%20Peter%20Worley.pdf

Worley, Peter. *The If Machine: 30 Lesson Plans for Teaching Philosophy*. (2nd edition). Bloomsbury, 2019b.

Worley, Peter. *The If Machine: Philosophical Enquiry in the Classroom*. Bloomsbury, 2011.

Worley, Peter. *The If Odyssey: A Philosophical Journey through Greek Myth and Storytelling for 8-16-Year-Olds*. Bloomsbury, 2012.

Worley, Peter. *The Philosophy Shop: Ideas, Activities and Questions to Get People, Young and Old, Thinking Philosophically*. Independent Thinking Press, 2012.

Worley, Peter and Andrew Day. *Thoughtings: Puzzles, Problems and Paradoxes in Poetry to Think With*. Independent Thinking Press, 2012.

About the Author

Peter Worley studied philosophy at University College London (2000), then completed an MA in philosophy at Birkbeck College, London (2004), and began a PhD in 'Plato and pedagogy' at King's College London (2009). He is the co-CEO and co-founder of *The Philosophy Foundation*, a registered charity that aims to bring philosophy into the public sphere, particularly education. He was President of *SOPHIA: The European foundation for the advancement of doing philosophy with children* from 2014–2018, and has been a Visiting Research Associate at King's College London since 2015. He has published many books, beginning with the bestselling *The If Machine* for Bloomsbury in 2011, with a second edition printed in 2019. His books have been translated into numerous languages from Danish to Korean. He has written and presented widely on doing philosophy in schools and has been training philosophers, teachers and educators in doing Philosophical Enquiry since 2007. He lives in London with his wife, fellow co-CEO and co-founder of *The Philosophy Foundation*, Emma Worley MBE, and their daughter, Katy. Peter is currently a PhD candidate at Sheffield University.